C000129579

BATTLE CHARACTERS
through the ages

Will's Cigarettes

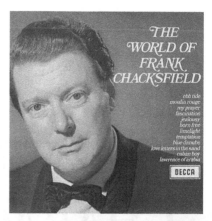

THE WORLD OF FRANK CHACKSFIELD

ebb tide
moulin rouge
my prayer
fascination
jealousy
born free
limelight
temptation
blue danube
love letters in the sand
cuban boy
lawrence of arabia

DECCA

THE HON. LIEUT.-GENERAL JAMES MURRAY.
From a print of about the year 1775.

By kind permission of the Clarendon Press, Oxford.

BATTLE
CHARACTERS
through the ages

George Kiloh

The Battle and District Historical Society

Also published by the Battle and District Historical Society:
George Kiloh, *The Brave Remembered,* 2015
Keith Foord and Neil Clephane-Cameron, *1066 and the Battle of Hastings,* 2015, 2016, 2018
Keith Foord, *Conquest to Dissolution 1067–1538,* 2019
Keith Foord, *BC to 1066,* 2020
Neil Clephane-Cameron, *1066 Malfosse Walk,* new ed. 2020

Copyright © Battle and District Historical Society 2021

ISBN: 978-1-903099-10-0

First published in the UK by
The Battle and District Historical Society
www.battlehistorysociety.co.uk

All rights reserved. No part of this publication may be reproduced, stored in a retrieval system, or transmitted in any form or by any means, electronic, mechanical, photocopying, recording or otherwise, without prior permission in writing from the Society.

Design and setting by Helm Information
amandahelm@uwclub.net

Contents

❦

Preface

Few small places will have more interesting people to commemorate than the Sussex town of Battle, along with its surrounding villages. We have painters and authors, actors, campaigners of various sorts, kings and scientists – and some mysteries. There is even a martyr from the Elizabethan age. Not all were worthy people, of course, and we've had our fair share of the misbehaved.

This book picks out most of those worthy of notice, even if very few make it to the *Dictionary of National Biography* (but one provided no fewer than 469 entries to that august publication).

The town is at the centre of fifteen other parishes, each with its own history. Almost all of them supplied characters for this book. What are now the much larger towns of Bexhill and Hastings have been excluded because of their size.

Most of the text derives from work done by members of the Battle and District Historical Society, and that work is listed at the end, before the index: apart from articles by the editor there are contributions by Neil Clephane-Cameron, Georgina Doherty, Keith Foord, Adrian and Sarah Hall and Charlotte Moore. Peter Greene and Keith Foord have done invaluable work on the illustrations. The essays on Sir Norman Moore and on Ben Leigh Smith have been kindly provided by Charlotte Moore. These and other sources can be found before the index.

All these articles have been re-edited, taking account of suggestions by the BDHS Research Group. In addition I am particularly grateful for the help of my wife Margaret and Amanda Helm.

Pictures and poems used are acknowledged where possible. If by chance I have missed any that should have been acknowledged, my apologies. I will do my best to remedy matters in any subsequent edition. The publisher is a registered charity with the objective of educating the public in the history of Battle and the surrounding area. This includes investigation, discussion and publication of matters relating to that objective. Any surplus from one BDHS publication is reinvested, and no officer, member or author of a publication receives any financial remuneration. BDHS policy is that its publications together should not result in a surplus.

Perhaps needless to say, any opinions expressed in this book are mine. And so are any mistakes that you find.

We could do with other small areas telling us more about their interesting people.

George Kiloh

Battle, Sussex
2021

1
The Naughties

There are naughty men everywhere, but perhaps you wouldn't expect to find Captain Hook as a vicar of a Sussex village, or a bank going bankrupt because directors made a silly investment in their brother, or a multiple fraudster posing as a minister in two continents and in almost every religious denomination you can think of, or an exiled king trying to start a revolution at home so that he could return. There are naughty women too: few of them made headlines in earlier times but two are here.

The original Captain Hook?

❧

John Williams Maher
(c. 1805–1851)

Firirst there was Captain Hook, or just possibly there wasn't. Everyone knows Hook, the menacing pirate from J.M. Barrie's *Peter Pan* and the star of a Disney film of 1953. There is one real-life candidate for him: John Williams Maher, rector of Brede for nine years from 1841; after graduation from Cambridge he had been curate at Brighouse in the West Riding. He presents a mystery. He was much liked at Brede and took a very active role in local affairs and was married to an Irish woman (who reverted to her maiden name after his death).

His oddity was that he had lost a hand and wore a metal hook where it had been. The reason for this was unclear, or at least it wasn't publicised until well after his death. His mind gave way in 1850. He sold his farm stock that autumn and was then confined to a lunatic asylum where he died in the following February.

The stories came out much later. In 1923 the *Sussex Express* contained a report based on someone having found a painting of Maher. It said that there were many strange stories about him, and that before taking Holy Orders he appears to have led the life of a pirate on the South American coast.

Oddly, it goes on to say that even his preparation for the ministry and his subsequent installation as Rector of Brede seem to have secured by shady means. It is unclear what is meant by 'shady means', for he was a Sussex man (of Irish extraction on his father's side, who had married at Heathfield, as he did) and he had a Cambridge degree. He bought the advowson of the parish from his immediate predecessor, as the latter was leaving the parish.

His earlier life had indeed been interesting and is by no means

The Rev. John Williams Maher © Dr John Crook, St George's, Brede. The artist may have kindly provided his missing hand.

clear to us. One account, from shortly after his death, states that at the age of thirteen, in about 1818, he had gone to South America to help in the rebellions there; that before going to Cambridge in 1829 he had written an account of his experiences; and that while he was away his father had been killed in a duel. This author attributes his insanity to the privations endured during the South American rebellions that lasted up to 1820. But there is a hint elsewhere that he may have been at Westminster School, maybe at the same time as he was said to be in or near South America. If he left school at 18 (and it may have been earlier) and didn't go to Cambridge until he was 29, he left an unexplained gap. If his thirteen-year-old time in South America had been so terrible he would have been unlikely to risk it again, so his visits southward probably help to fill the later gap rather than his being there at a very young age. He would naturally wish to avoid any suggestion of piracy. Quite apart from its inconsistency with priesthood it was a capital offence.

Peter Pan dates from 1904, and its author J M Barrie had been at Brede Place earlier as one of the long line of literary figures entertained either by Stephen Crane or by Moreton Frewen[*] and his wife Clara; it seems unlikely that it was by the Frewens. If Brede people knew

---

[*] see chapter 11.

of Maher's early life it would have been then that Barrie was told of it. No doubt they knew more than what got into print, but equally a fifty-year old tale might well have gathered some embellishment.

With characteristic reticence the press reported nothing relevant until 1930, nearly 80 years after Maher died:

> The character of Captain Hook was inspired by Reverend John Maher, a preacher at St. George's parish in Brede …. At first glance, Maher appeared to be a small-town Reverend who happened to have a hook in place of his left hand. He told everyone he lost it in a coach accident. No one had any reason to doubt his story until a man named Smith came to town and revealed that Maher lost his left hand in his previous career as a pirate. Apparently, Maher had a pretty successful career until he decided to strand his partner, Smith, in the Caribbean, return to England, and become a man of the cloth. Smith tracked down his old friend and set out to blackmail him. The pressure was too much for Maher, and paranoia drove him mad. [*grammatically corrected*]

If Smith did come to Brede it may well have been in 1850, when Maher began to miss appointments. Another investigator writes:

> Far from having lost his hand under the wheel of the Oxford mail coach, it had, in fact, been unceremoniously and violently removed when the good Mr Maher had been illegally boarding a tobacco clipper in the Caribbean with a view to stealing the ship and its cargo; for before taking Holy Orders and buying the living of Brede, the Reverend John Maher had indeed been a pirate!

To have engaged in piracy before going to Cambridge is certainly possible, given the gap referred to above. Even when we know that piracy on the high seas was a capital offence and that the Royal Navy patrolled the Caribbean (but less so South America) this may well be true. Of course the Maher story might be an invention, but the idea of Captain Hook had to come from somewhere. It may be relevant that the fictional character had been to a famous English public school, retaining some of the appearance and behaviour of such people, and was a raconteur of some repute. That certainly fits Maher. Hook's falling out with fellow-pirate Smee (a name close to Smith) suggests the kind of enmity described in the first quotation above. But that only reflects what Barrie was told.

The pluralist Vicar

Edward Craven Hawtrey
(1789–1862)

ew people are aware of Hawtrey and they might be surprised to find him of note in the Battle area – or, indeed, to find him there at all. He was an intellectual cleric and teacher, highly regarded as such by the many who came into contact with him. He wrote a number of learned books.

DR. HAWTREY HEARING REPETITION.
" Oh, I see what it is : you haven't learnt it at all."
From a sketch by Francis Tarver.

One doubts whether any of his contacts would be in Ewhurst, however, where he was rector from 1835 to 1853. Indeed Hawtrey himself can't have been there very often.

He is on these pages because he would take the medal – if there was one it would be made of lead – for having so many jobs that it is most unlikely that he was able to perform all of them fully. This was once common among Church of England vicars, and it was only in the nineteenth century that steps were taken to limit it (nowadays vicars often legitimately serve a number of adjoining parishes).

Apart from his years at Cambridge (1808–12) Hawtrey spent most of his life at Eton as pupil, teacher then headmaster (1834–53). He was highly regarded as a teacher. Gladstone, one of his pupils, said of him: "He … for the first time inspired me with a desire to learn and to do."

Given the then state of travel he must have relied very heavily on overworked curates at Ewhurst, which was a long way away from Eton. Even now the nearest station is at Robertsbridge, some four miles away, and that opened only in 1851.

In 1853 he was appointed Provost of Eton, and the position of rector of Eton came with it. Perhaps that finally persuaded him to give up Ewhurst. On the other hand the rector held the advowson of Mapledurham in Oxfordshire and he was duly appointed vicar there. On his death he became the last person to be buried in Eton College chapel.

He was the son of a vicar and fathered two more. Quite apart from his pluralism, as head of Eton he appointed a son to a teaching post. A grandson became nationally well-known as a comedian, playwright and producer, knighted in 1922, the year before his death. (The actor Charles Hawtrey, of *Carry On* fame, was no relation and took the Hawtrey name soon after the grandson died.)

The failed Banker

❦

Tilden Smith
(1799–1880)

Today failed bankers seem to retire with huge benefits whether successful or not, but in the mid-nineteenth century it could also be so.

The Hastings banking crisis broke in 1857. It centred on the Smith family of Mountfield and in particular on Tilden Smith. He had what may seem today an unusual first name but it wasn't uncommon in Sussex and Kent and was perhaps originally a surname. His father had been one of the founders of the Hastings Old Bank in 1791, and the family had grown richer on its success. By the 1820s it had a branch at banks and three others. The young Tilden also became a director, as did his brother Francis, and he was able to build a large house at Vinehall in Mountfield and to lease the old and also large Great Sanders house at Sedlescombe.

It was family loyalty that caught him out. Another brother, Richard, was a local farmer, in difficulties even before the hop harvest failures of 1847 and 1848 and nearby years. He appealed to the bank for help.

Tilden and Francis being two of the four directors, the bank lent Richard £116 15s 6d, secured on his quite extensive lands. It appears that other directors were not consulted. One would think that such a small sum was unimportant but calculations of its present-day value can be as high as £345,000.

The loan did not save Richard from bankruptcy, which duly happened in June 1857. Four days later the bank closed its doors, never to reopen them. A sorry state then revealed itself. There was about £25,000 circulating in notes; liabilities were less than £150,000 but assets only £78,600. (Richard also owed £700 to the Battle Poor

Law Guardians, and his bankruptcy caused them difficulty too.)

Another bank stepped in, and the creditors of the Old Bank suffered small loss. The saviour was the London and County, a major bank of the time and an ancestor of the National Westminster. They took on all the staff of the Old Bank and opened permanent branches at Battle, Hawkhurst, Robertsbridge and St Leonards. In Battle their temporary home was opposite the George Inn; they soon moved across the street.

Tilden Smith was a survivor. He had to sell Vinehall and end his lease of Great Sanders, but he moved to become a farmer just outside Battle. He left a large sum of money.

Hastings Old Bank note, 1847
from www.spink.com/lot/12035805

The wife-killing Doctor

❧

Charles West Roberts
(1827–1866)

In December 1861 a major incident arose at Battle. It ended without prosecution but there should have been one for manslaughter if not for murder.

The Watts family, physicians to the area for about a century, were backing out of medicine but still owned their practice, and in 1861 they engaged Roberts. He had been practising in Kent and seemed to fit the bill. As befitted his status, he moved into a fine nearly-new house at 5 St Mary's Villas, to the south of the town, with large estate gardens in front of it and easy access to the station.

He and his wife Eliza already had a daughter, and a son had arrived just before they came to Battle. As was only too common at that time the mother fell ill; we don't know the nature of her complaint. Roberts prescribed laudanum. This derivate of opium was a common drug of the day. If carefully managed in small doses it suppressed pain without side-effects but there are many examples of addiction, for the death of some of whom – Elizabeth Barrett Browning being one – laudanum might be blamed. We don't know what doses Roberts gave, and her condition grew worse.

He then gave her brandy; she became much worse. Her sister came to see her and later said that on a particular day Roberts had given his wife a whole bottle of brandy; he said half a bottle.

In desperation he called in two other doctors. They were shocked at her treatment and said that that amount of spirits added to the laudanum was certain to cause death. They could do nothing. They were almost certainly right, for very soon she died.

At the inquest the doctors gave evidence that Roberts was drunk throughout their attendance. They stated that the quantity of brandy administered to his wife was likely to be lethal when combined with the laudanum. In defence, Roberts claimed that his wife had died of a heart defect, but the other doctors could find no evidence for this. Manslaughter would seem to be the minimal verdict that the coroner's jury could return but they chose accidental death. When they gave the verdict, they added that Roberts's conduct had been "extremely censurable". One observer shouted that there was not much chance of his Battle practice continuing – and it didn't. He left very soon. He didn't live long, for he died in Somerset less than five years later, aged only 39. His probate record describes him as a surgeon so he might still have been in practice.

A delinquent Vicar

ళ్యా౪ం

Robert Richard Duke
(1833–1900)

Welle expect our priests to be pillars of the community but Robert Duke, the first vicar of Netherfield, is known for his piety but for quite different reasons. During the course of his life he was declared bankrupt, then charged with indecent assault and jailed for nine months.

Duke was a son and a brother of Battle doctors, and his LLB was from Cambridge. He obtained the living at Netherfield in 1868 when it split from the ecclesiastical parish of Battle, and at the beginning of that year he preached his first sermon in the splendid if restrained new Gothic church. After this promising start, however, his tenure was short. Then it was downhill all the way. By November he had performed his last baptism and very soon resigned.

The reason for this became clear when, in the following March, Duke was declared bankrupt. He was the proprietor of the Oxford and Cambridge private hotel in Warrior Square, St Leonards, which had proved too heavy a burden, 'not having realised my expectations as an hotel'. This seems slightly odd in that St Leonards was a popular coastal area and had a substantial hotel trade, but there are many reasons why bankruptcy might happen and we can only guess at the cause on this occasion. His unsecured creditors were owed £10,241; they included members of his family and James Watts of Battle.

In November 1869 he was discharged from bankruptcy and for a while things looked up. In the 1871 census he appears as the curate of No Man's Heath in Warwickshire. By 1876 he was a curate at Smarden in Kent.

But at the beginning of 1880 ominous signs were published – not locally but in newspapers elsewhere, including Liverpool, Edinburgh and County Wexford. Clearly this was big news, even if the local press was too reticent to mention it. His last official event at Smarden had been at the end of December 1879 and in the next month he was charged with indecently assaulting a footman in the service of someone, perhaps appropriately, reported as General Cannon.

The papers that ran the story called the accused Albert rather than Robert, and rather later Alexander. (Was he trying to avoid identification by colleagues?) The alleged victim was everywhere named as Louis, with a widely variable surname: Marat, Morrell, Macrot, Marot, Mavet. Unable to find bail, Duke was remanded in custody pending the next Quarter Sessions; on the grounds that local prejudice was so strong, the case was referred to the Old Bailey.

He came up for trial late in April 1880. Despite declarations of good character by the vicars of Smarden and a neighbouring parish, the jury found him guilty and the judge sent him down for nine months; he went first to Newgate prison and then within days back to Canterbury prison. What happened thereafter is unclear for he makes only shadowy appearances in the public records. He seems to have become a reformed character or at least more discreet, as he remained in Holy Orders. The 1891 census records him living at Chipping Barnet in Hertfordshire. In 1897 he was a curate, this time at Weston-sub-Edge in Gloucestershire. He died in Devon, a long way from Sussex and Kent.

The phoney Priest with three names

❧❧❧

James Joseph Crouch
(1838–?)

As if the above were not enough, the naughtiest person in this account has yet to emerge. Possibly he never killed anyone but he was a fraud and a thief and probably a bigamist. He had intelligence and must have had great charm and guile, being able to talk his way round and convince many people, including women, of his sincerity and good will. From what we know he was caught only a few times, but almost certainly we don't know all.

Crouch was a son of a Mountfield labourer and a washerwoman. Admitted to the Battle workhouse in 1851, he had enough education there to make acting and religion his life's work, but not in the conventional way. With charm and eloquence he felt that he could get away with anything. He was wrong: he went to prison at least three times.

At the workhouse he encouraged others to believe that he wanted to pursue his interest in Roman Catholicism. Having become a Catholic and then released he went to Rome, but after three years in a seminary he was expelled for 'vicious behaviour'. He returned to Britain to begin a career of being a phoney priest, in virtually all denominations.

First he posed as a novitiate at Father Ignatius's monastery at Norwich but was found to be 'instilling bad principles into the minds of the brethren' with his 'damnable doctrines', and removed. He took a large sum of money with him and became a chaplain on a ship taking emigrants to Australia.

His conduct on board was hardly priestly. He seduced one woman and paid so much unwanted attention to others that they stripped, tarred and feathered him. On arrival he was engaged as a curate but his papers were found to be false, so he served three months of imprisonment. After he came back to Britain he couldn't resist going back to the Battle workhouse as the Reverend Arthur Morton; he was recognised but gave everyone the slip. He was then engaged as a Baptist minister at Stony Stratford, where he borrowed money and left without repaying it.

This was his trade mark: wherever he went he left debts that were not honoured, removed articles from where he stayed and failed to pay his bills.

The authorities caught up with him but it took them well over a decade. He was serving as a curate at Worcester when his rector saw an advertisement for a man exactly fitting his description. He checked Morton's certificates and found some erasures. Morton tried to snatch his London MA certificate from him but failed. The rector checked on the ordination records of his claimed diocese of Bath and Wells. The answer was that no such person had been ordained in the year concerned. Further examination showed that the certification was that of another man, partly forged to include the miscreant's name. He must have stolen it from somewhere he'd stayed.

At the Worcester assizes in 1872 he was sentenced to 6½ years penal servitude for theft and, after that, to seven years' police supervision. Even then he wasn't done. He surfaced again.

As Thomas Keating, in 1886 he was pursued by the Dublin police for impersonating a priest, and late in that year he was found guilty of obtaining money by false pretences, being sentenced to eighteen months imprisonment with hard labour. The formal charge was that he 'by various false and fraudulent means, obtained certain sums of money from clergymen and the Priests' Protection Society by representing that from the age of 14 years he had been professing the Roman Catholic religion, and had subsequently been an ordained clergyman of that Church, and afterwards embraced the Protestant faith'.

He was released early in the following September on grounds of ill-health and was apparently intending to go to Australia. However it was reported in court that a son lived in America and perhaps that is where he finally went. Given his multiplicity of aliases it seems unlikely that public records would tell us more.

An improper Earl

❧⟡❧

Jack Needham,
Second Earl of Kilmorey
(1787–1880)

Next there is Kilmorey. People thought him improper. In the eighteenth century his behaviour might not have been noticed at all but in the different climate of the mid-nineteenth it was.

The tithe survey of 1860 shows him as owning a little land at Battle – less than half an acre on the east side of Hastings Road south of the Black Horse – but also occupying about 44 acres, based at Little Hemingfold. The origin of his association with Battle is unclear and may have had some connection with his private life (his leased land belonged to Anna Lamb, young widow of Beaufort).* He seems to have lived at Battle from time to time, but not to have been in the town for long. He first appears in local records in 1858 when he arranged for the local poor to receive meat, bread and clothing, at a generous average of 12s each and with a total outlay of £208.

Jack was the son of the first earl, a landowner and a General. His father thought him so unreliable that he put into trust his huge Irish estate near Newry rather than let him take charge of it. That did not stop Jack from having a very long wall put up around the 55,000-acre estate as work for locals beset by the Irish famine.

Jack moved around Middlesex and other southern counties, buying and selling properties, quite apart from numerous trips abroad. In 1814 he married Jane Cunninghame of County Wicklow and they had children, but by 1835 they had separated (but never divorced). He took up to living openly with Priscilla Anne Hoste, whom sources say was his legal ward. She was about 19 and he was

---

*   See Chapter 2

48 when they eloped. Relations with his family broke down.

Priscilla was the second daughter of Sir William Hoste, a Norfolk man and a well-known naval captain who took part in most of the sea battles of the Revolutionary and Napoleonic wars. He is best known for securing the island of Lissa (now Viš in Croatia) which became a British colony for a few years.[*]

In 1844 they had a child whom Jack acknowledged as his. He set up his mistress in a house next to his with a tunnel between the two. They had no other child and she died young, in 1854. Her mausoleum was at first at Brompton Cemetery but as Jack moved around so did the mausoleum (though never to Battle). It came finally to rest in St Margaret's Road, Twickenham. The cost of its original erection, in terms of purchasing power, was about £95,000 in 2019 values.

The second mention of Jack local to Battle is in the minutes of the local Board of Health in October 1859, when he offered to build a drinking fountain on what is now the Abbey Green. This was a generous gesture, and there is little doubt that one would have been useful. It is clear that the fountain removed in 1919 was not his and dated from early in the new century.

Known by his family as Black Jack or the wicked earl, whether he was wicked or not depends on your definition. When he died he was buried in the mausoleum next to Priscilla. Whatever people thought of his behaviour he was clearly devoted to her.

The Kilmorey Mausoleum.
Photo: Maxwell Hamilton.

---

[*]   The revived cricket club there is the Sir William Hoste Club

The exiled King of Portugal

ॐ

Miguel I
(1802–1866)

S o far we haven't mentioned the only king ever to have lived at Battle, but his conduct deserves his inclusion here. He was at Battle for an even shorter time than Kilmorey.

Miguel was an ambitious and very silly young man who threw away his prospect of reaching the throne peacefully and by consent.

His whole life was controversial. After the peace of 1815, Portugal was to split from its colony Brazil, where the first emperor was a son of the Portuguese king. Miguel, the other son, was heir to the European part and to the rest of the Portuguese empire, which stretched as far as Goa and Macau and had very substantial interests in Africa. To rule it would have been a real honour and no doubt Miguel looked forward to doing so.

His father had returned to Portugal after the expulsion of the French in 1813 and he moved towards the more liberal régimes being toyed with in continental Europe: he gave the country a constitution. Miguel disagreed, and early in the 1820s he attempted a coup that failed. The king ticked him off but he tried again. Then the king told him that a third attempt would mean exile and that the succession would move elsewhere. In 1824 that is exactly what happened. With the consent of the Cortes (parliament) the king disqualified him. His other child being Emperor of Brazil, he appointed as heiress the Emperor's daughter Maria. Then he died, in 1826. If Miguel had held off he would then lawfully have been king.

Princess Maria lived in Brazil and it would take time for her to reach Portugal. Miguel acted fast, no doubt using as an argument that a mere girl of seven years should not be a reigning queen.

Being an outright reactionary he obtained strong support from landowners and the Catholic Church, for they were suffering difficulties under the constitution. Agreement was reached through the Cortes that Maria should rule, with Miguel as regent. One account suggests that they were to marry, which seems more than a little odd given that he was her uncle in a strongly Catholic country.

Ex-king Miguel in later life,

True to form, Miguel stopped Maria from landing in Portugal and assumed full power, ruling as an autocrat. This act was not popular with the prosperous middle class, and the country's main overseas customers were disturbed at the potential loss of trade as civil unrest arose.

The British tried to stay formally out of these troubles, and their men couldn't get involved without formal consent under the Foreign Enlistment Act. So Captain Charles Napier took command of the Portuguese navy under the name Carlos de Ponza (chosen from his exploit in occupying the strategic island of Ponza near Naples during the recent wars). He was indeed crossed off the Navy List for his actions, which included commanding an army to take back northern Portugal for Maria, but he later resumed an imaginative and successful naval career.

In 1834 Miguel suffered his final defeat and signed the capitulation of Evora. He was to leave Portugal, never to return, or even to go to Spain, and to cease all activity that would disturb his country's peace. In return he would have an annual pension of £2,000. One source puts the present-day value at the lowest at about £170,000 but on other criteria it climbs to about £2,000,000. It looks like a comfortable sum. Needless to say, he did not keep his promises. Denouncing the agreement, his pension ceased.

To 1851 he attempted comebacks, but then his last attempt failed. He was living at Battle, in the large mid-eighteenth century house called Rose Green in an area now covered by the Glengorse estate. Why he chose to move there from Bexhill is unclear, but the Websters of the Abbey needed a better income. It may also be that the Government felt that as far as possible he ought to be kept out of London.

Later that year he married into a mediatised* family in Germany and stayed in that country. The line of Portuguese kings has died out, so Miguel's descendants are now the legitimate claimants to the throne. So perhaps he won after all.

* This term applies to the rulers of the small states that under the Holy Roman Empire reported directly to the emperor. They lost their independence when the empire was abandoned in 1805 but were allowed to keep a number of privileges.

An adulterous Wife

❧❧❧

Elizabeth Vassall, later Webster, later Holland
(1770–1845)

nd now to one of the only two naughty women recorded, and on the first of them there is much information. Of course she was wealthy, at least at first, and ended up as the wife of a well-known peer and hostess of political meetings. But her first married life couldn't have been happy.

Elizabeth Vassall was heiress to a considerable fortune based on slavery and sugar in the West Indies. We don't know how she got to know Sir Godfrey Webster, the fourth baronet of his line, who had succeeded his uncle in the baronetcy. They married in 1786. She was only 15 and he 38. They would have three children.

Marriage to Godfrey can't have been an easy matter. He couldn't live at Battle Abbey because under the will of his uncle, the second baronet, the Abbey was his aunt's for life and she was to outlive him by ten years. In retrospect that was a good thing because he had plans to knock down what remained of it and build a great new house. Godfrey and Elizabeth had to live elsewhere: at Rose Green, the property mentioned above. It was probably a much better place to live than the crumbling abbey, however.

Godfrey was generally thought unstable if not approaching madness. He gambled heavily, sought women of less than perfect virtue, and had a terrible temper. He made scarcely any impact in Parliament where he sat from 1786 to 1790 and from 1796 until his death. To maintain his reckless lifestyle he had to sell parts of his estate. Nevertheless he still had money, particularly after his marriage.

Elizabeth had grown up in a metropolitan atmosphere and disliked Battle, a rural backwater. It is more than likely that she had begun to dislike Godfrey too. For five years from 1791 they escaped for much of their time to the mainland, mainly to Italy.

Elizabeth, Lady Webster, by Louis Gauffier, 1794.

Occasionally Godfrey had to return to England, and Elizabeth took full advantage of her temporary liberation. She seems to have had affairs with Thomas Pelham (soon to be the second Earl of Chichester), by whom she may have had a daughter, and with a son of the Duke of Marlborough. Then she met Henry Holland. He was already a baron, having succeeded his father at the age of one. Together they had a child, the evidence of whom was sufficient to support Godfrey's claim for divorce.

Elizabeth must have breathed more than one sigh of relief and did not contest the action.

In those days divorce was rare and attracted public attention, even when an undefended Bill was briefly brought before both Houses of Parliament.

Many would have shied away even from this small publicity but not Godfrey, probably because of the large amount of money at stake: he ended with additional capital of £16,000 (in present-day purchasing power this is over £1.5 million.) Given his proclivities, even that didn't get him out of difficulty. Moreover he had been a naughty boy probably much more frequently than had his ex-wife had been a naughty girl. Prone to mental difficulties likely to have arisen from venereal disease, he shot himself dead in 1800.

Meanwhile Lady Holland – as Elizabeth became very shortly – made well of herself. She seems to have suffered none of the indignities usually heaped on wives divorced on grounds of their adultery.

Henry Holland was well-connected in the Whig party, being the nephew of Charles James Fox, the great antagonist of the younger Pitt. He was a minister in the 1806–07 'ministry of all the talents' and a very strong opponent of the reactionary governments of 1807–30. He was a minister again for almost all the years between 1834 and 1840.

Elizabeth was devoted to him. They had six more children and she made a name for herself as a society hostess at Holland House in Kensington. According to the cleric and wit Sydney Smith she was strong-willed, imperious and prone to deep hatreds and affections, but very generous and warm-hearted. She was famously an excellent hostess.

No wonder she and Godfrey had not got on.

Despite all this, the name Vassall survived. Holland attached it to his own family name, though his son, destined to be the last baron, could not continue it. It stayed with the Websters: the last baronet's son had it.

The last naughty Webster

❦

Lucy Webster
(1900–89)

Lucy Webster was the elder daughter of Sir Augustus, the last baronet of Battle and a descendant of Lady Holland. Her reputation remains dubious.

Lucy Webster. From the *Daily Mirror*, 14 May 1919, aged 18.
shown in connection with victory celebrations; (improved by Peter Greene from the British Newspaper Archive).

Her brother died in the First World War and as the elder of two sisters she became heir to Battle Abbey. After learning what had to be done to maintain an estate she appears to have been ready to take over, two years after her father's death in 1923, though by then some of it had been sold by his executors and effective control was in the hands of trustees.

Shortly after his death she went on a long tour of east Africa,

23

returning in April 1924, but earlier she had been active as captain of the Battle Girl Guides, arranging fund-raising events for them at the Abbey. Lucy lit the November bonfires in 1922 and 1924, on the second occasion dressed as Guy Fawkes and coming on horseback at the head of the procession. In 1925, while living at Tollgates in Battle, she said that she was renting a Mayfair flat for the 'London season' and she appeared in local papers at least up to 1927, when she gave away her sister in marriage – but not after 1929. Even that last mention may be a formality, the legal case in question having been presented by the trustees. A later record states that her sister Evelyn acted on her behalf in all local matters from 1934.

She developed an alarming local reputation. Local rumour insists that she ran naked down Battle High Street, and she appears to have had a remarkable sexual appetite that at one point left her with a venereal disease.

She was strongly religious, a characteristic not easily compatible with nymphomania, and she asked to be certified insane. She was interned for the rest of her long life. Among older Battle people the quip is that her departure made a lot of local men very disappointed.

The 1939 Register has her at Bryn-y-Neuadd Mental Hospital at Llanfairfechan in Caernarvonshire. She was to die at St Andrew's (mental) Hospital, Northampton, where much earlier 'Captain Hook' had died.

Lucy had always been a little bit of a problem. After her mother's death she was looked after by an aunt as guardian, who had a difficult time. Lucy found concentration difficult but had great if transient enthusiasms. She was not interested in her education. She had no sense of financial responsibility and in this she shared an unfortunate trait of too many of her ancestors. ESBHRO records that her aunt found Lucy trying – 'Lucy on the loose is like a steam engine with the valve blown off', but had affection and hopes for her; in 1921 she wrote "she's still very young and rather erratic, but she is the right stuff and after all she is only 20".

The trouble is that stories of this kind can be embellished and true facts concealed or distorted. To be certified she must have been insane by medical standards, irrespective of any request she might have made.

2
Writers

❦

T his area has been associated with probably more notable artists of the word than most other places of its size. Indeed, it's a little hard to choose among them. And of course there are some less well-known.

There are writers with Battle connections, some closer than others, who are not in this account: among them are Warwick Deeping (1877–1950), D K Broster (1877–1950), Reginald Pound (1894–1991), Patience Strong (1907–90) and Nigel Balchin (1908–70). Alfred Tennyson's connection is thin, though he did write *Show-day at Battle Abbey, 1876* as the prologue to his poetic drama *Harold*.

Mrs Beeton's Predecessor

❧❧

Eliza Acton
(1799–1859)

Mrs Beeton is famous and she has unfairly overtaken Eliza Acton as a food writer. From all accounts Acton was a more imaginative, careful and experimental cook.

Until her time the cookery books on offer were almost always for professional cooks, usually women supervised by their landladies. In contrast she addressed the needs of married women running houses for their families without the employment of professional cooks. All of them sold well. She produced four such books, all of which have appeared under varied titles: Modern Cookery for Private Families, The English Bread Book, Invalid Cookery and The Elegant Economist.

If you look at cookery books by earlier authors they are remarkably unhelpful when it comes to weight, volume, treatment and temperature. Acton's were the first to take the reader through the preparation and cooking processes, specifying the type and weight or volume of the ingredients. They paid respect to what was available at particular seasons but also reflected the fact that the country was now importing all kinds of foodstuffs that were new to the public. She included dishes that respected the sometimes different requirements of Catholic and Jewish cooks. She had tested every recipe, unlike Mrs Beeton, who appears to have stolen many of her recipes and tasted very few. In due course she sold her rights in the books to Longman's for the sum of £300. Comparing historic and current values is never easy, but in terms of income that would represent at least £320,000 today.

Born at Battle, part of the locally respected and prosperous Slatter trading family, she spent her early life in Suffolk where her father was

Eliza Acton

an Ipswich brewer (until bankruptcy claimed him, whereupon he did the traditional thing of decamping to Calais).

In 1816 Eliza and a colleague founded 'a boarding school for young ladies' in a village near Ipswich. This didn't last, though we don't know why. In 1819 she and a sister were running a new school near Woodbridge, which appears to have lasted at least five years.

At first she wrote poetry, publishing in 1826. She took up cookery because, it's said, the London publisher William Longman, who had retailed her first poetry book, declined to take on another and advised her to move to cookery. We don't know whether he was aware of her interest in cooking or whether it was simply a traditional sexist call for women to return to the kitchen, but it certainly had its effect.

Eliza was probably never very well, and she began to ail towards the end of the 1850s. In 1859 she died at Snowdon House in Hampstead. She is buried in the churchyard there. She never married.

The slightly risqué Writer

❧✦☙

Violet Fane
(1843–905)

F ane was a minor nineteenth-century writer who achieved some
popularity and who is now almost, but not quite, forgotten.
In the nineteenth century some people felt that her view of
morality was perhaps questionable. But it helped sales.

Her background was a little odd. Her father was Charles Lamb,
heir to the Beauport baronetcy, and the story goes that he met her
future mother Anna Charlotte Gray by accident at Selsey in 1842,
when aged 18 she was about to drown herself in the sea. She claimed
that she was being pressured to join an Indian princely harem. They
eloped and Anna became pregnant with the child who, after their
marriage, would become Marie Montgomerie Lamb, later known by
her *nom de plume* Violet Fane; she would say that her mother was a
gypsy. Charles was hardly a reliable husband, and he would never
inherit the baronetcy, dying (it is thought of syphilis) in 1856.

The 1851 census records Anna living at Beauport, but in 1861 she
lived in Kent with her four children. Her 41 acres at Battle in 1860
must have been a form of agreement with the Lambs that she leave
the area but have an income. She returned later.

Marie's first marriage was to an Irish landowner, Henry Sydenham
Singleton, in 1864, and they had four children. He died in 1893 and
she married Sir Philip Henry Wodehouse Currie GCB (later Lord
Currie of Hawley), the British ambassador to the Ottoman empire;
this meant a move to what was then Constantinople.*

She took the pen name *Violet Fane* from Benjamin Disraeli's

---

* Ambassadors then were not the Crown's only representatives in foreign lands:
only eight had that esteemed title, in the countries historically most important
to the UK.

Violet Fane, engraved by Edward William Stodart, from *Poems by Violet Fane*, 1892

Vivien Grey. Her success was no doubt partly due to her good looks but also because she had an engaging manner and an imaginative use of words. In due course she was one of those who were regarded as part of Oscar Wilde's circle – indeed he mentioned her name when applying for a job in 1887. By then she had published only poetry.

She wrote under her pen-name but also under her second married name. As Violet Fane she wrote seven books of poetry, three novels and a translation from the French of the memoirs of a queen of Navarre, and two essays as Mary Currie. Her poetry is very much of her age, well-constructed and direct:

> Let me arise and open the gate,
>   To breathe the wild warm air of the heath,
> And to let in Love, and to let out Hate,
> And anger at living, and scorn of Fate,
>   To let in Life, and to let out Death.

Her books sold well but one cannot avoid the suspicion that sexual references had something to do with that, and *Denzil Place* survives as an example. Certainly she was no stranger to romantic passion, having had at least one premarital affair and multiple adulteries afterwards, including one with the poet Wilfred Scawen Blunt (by no means his only affair, either). Her readership was almost certainly female, for she tended to concentrate on female love – and given her experience that is understandable.

One modern critic writes that her writing has considerable power and that she showed skill in her poetry. To a modern ear her themes would be outdated, but – apart from a touch of racism – the slightly risqué nature of her work would be in no way unattractive. But few of her works now sell.

The young American Writer at Brede

❧❧

Stephen Crane
(1871–1900)

Crane was one of the English language's foremost writers, and lived at Brede Place in 1899–1900. His works mark the beginning of modern realistic and naturalistic writing in America.

He is particularly celebrated for *The Red Badge of Courage* (1895), a classic that realistically depicts fear and courage on the battlefield. H G Wells, who became his friend, noted that *The Red Badge of Courage* was welcomed with an 'orgy of praise' in England. In 1951 it was made into a well-received film, directed by John Huston.

During his short life Crane became intensely unpopular in his home country: "There seem so many of them in America who want to kill, bury and forget me purely out of unkindness and envy and—my unworthiness, if you choose". His early self-published book *Maggie: a Girl of the Streets* was a gritty, realistic look at life in New York's slums. It exposed lives that were inconsistent with the American myth, and puritanical objectors made many calls for censorship against him. This refrain was picked up by the New York establishment, which he scorned.

A *Guardian* review of 2014 placed *The Red Badge of Courage* 30th in the list of '100 best books'. In the same year the *New York Times* reviewed a biography of him and reminded readers that his image, 'America's first rock-star writer,' appeared on the album cover of The Beatles' *Sergeant Pepper's Lonely Hearts Club Band* (1967).

In America he lived an impoverished life of observed experience and experiment with his writing style. He had a 'clinical' attraction to the low life, frequenting bars and doss-houses to inform his realistic and socially uncomfortable writing. He lent money to and protected prostitutes, and became their penniless hanger-on. He started into journalism, but he could fall out with editors after finding his truthful reports manipulated by them. At that time editors practised what was called 'yellow journalism'; we are familiar with it here and now. With his fanatical love for the truth he hated it.

His unconventional poetry (*The Black Riders and other Lines* and *War is Kind*) and short stories such as 'The Open Boat', based on his personal experience of being shipwrecked, received much more acclaim after his death than during his life. In the twentieth century his writing was to make a deep impression on modernistic American writers, most clearly Ernest Hemingway. Robert McCrum of The *Guardian* said in 2014 that his influence had also been noted in Mailer's *The Naked and the Dead*, Heller's *Catch-22*, James Jones's *The Thin Red Line* and Karl Marlantes's *Matterhorn*. Hemingway's *A Farewell to Arms* is said to have some similarities to *The Red Badge of Courage*.

Finally Crane found and settled with the 'big blue eyed and reddish haired' Cora Stewart, an estranged wife and madame of a 'house of assignation' in Florida.

She was someone who could have been in Shaw's *Mrs. Warren's Profession*, but a rather more complicated version. She had not been poor and the brothel she ran at Jacksonville was far from squalid. It was there that she met Crane.

They first arrived in England early in 1897 on their way to Greece, where Stephen was to report for the *New York Journal* on the Greek–Turkish war of that year. Before they left there was a lunch at the Savoy where among others he met J M Barrie. Both he and Cora left England on 1 April, arriving at Piraeus nine days before Turkey declared war. Cora acted as a war correspondent in her own right. People assumed they were married although some remembered her as Mrs Stewart: Cora had failed to get a divorce.

British literary circles received Crane warmly during a short stay at Oxted at the end of June 1897. That area was home to numbers of idealistic members of the Fabian Society and writers such as Harold Frederic, Edmund Gosse, Ford Madox Ford, H G Wells and Edward

**Stephen Crane and Cora Stewart. At a garden party in the
grounds of Brede Rectory, August 1899**

Garnett. He also met Joseph Conrad in October 1897 – 'the start of
warm and endless friendship' said Crane. But by the end of that year
he and Cora were running out of money.

Early in 1898 he was offered a job to report on the Spanish–
American war and went back to the USA. He ran out of money and
Cora, left at Oxted, was also broke.

Communication between them was necessarily poor. She might
even have thought he had died, but he arrived back in England in
January 1899. Shortly after they moved to Brede Place with the help
of loans from family and friends.

The house had neither electricity nor indoor plumbing. Its sanitary
arrangements were of the 17th century.* The building was in very bad
condition, and Clara Frewen leased it to Crane for a peppercorn rent
on the basis that he and Cora would make a start on re-decoration.
Cora apparently struggled to make it liveable, somehow furnishing
a dozen or so rooms with very old furniture and colourful blankets.

Brede Place was often full of hangers-on, which wouldn't have
helped them financially. A strong camaraderie developed between

---

* For a picture of Brede Place and a description of its condition at the time, see
Chapter 8.

Crane, then 28, and the writers who lived nearby. These included Henry James (55), Joseph Conrad (43), H.G. Wells (33), and Ford Madox Ford (26). It is probable that a close friendship did not develop with James, who was much older, though they visited each other's houses and were members of the Mermaid Club, at the Mermaid Inn a few yards from James's house at Rye.

Crane was at Brede for about 15 months and at first he wrote intensely, but his health worsened. He was obviously dying from TB. Cora managed to get him to a clinic in Badenweiler in Germany for 'a cure'. A few days after arriving there he had severe pulmonary haemorrhages and was given terminal care with morphine injections. He died on 5 June 1900. In the ten years left to her Cora went back to Jacksonville to resume her previous occupation.

He had published five novels, two volumes of poetry, three short story collections, two books of war stories, and numerous works of short fiction as well as his reporting. Crane's reputation was developed and enhanced after his death by his writer friends, all of whom either published recollections or commented upon their time with Crane.

Ford wrote that Henry James grieved deeply over 'my young compatriot of genius'. Henry James wrote to H G Wells: 'You will have felt, as I have done, the miserable sadness of poor Crane's so precipitated and, somehow, so unnecessary extinction.' Later writers have called Crane one of the finest creative spirits of his time. Hemingway in *The Green Hills of Africa* wrote that: 'The good writers are Henry James, Stephen Crane, and Mark Twain. That's not the order they're good in. There is no order for good writers.'

> There was a man who lived a life of fire.
> Even upon the fabric of time,
> Where purple becomes orange
> And orange purple,
> This life glowed,
> A dire red stain, indelible;
> Yet when he was dead,
> He saw that he had not lived.

From *'The Black Riders and other Lines*

The best-selling Sussex writer

❧❧

Sheila Kaye-Smith
(1887–1956)

It would be hard to find an author so different from those above as Sheila Kaye-Smith. Her books concentrated often on the Sussex that she had known all her life but that didn't prevent them from large sales across the world.

Although born at St Leonards, she maintained close contacts with Battle and the surrounding area. Her father was Edward Smith, later Kaye-Smith, who came to Battle as a doctor in 1867, taking the house at 22 Upper Lake. He and his wife had their daughter Annie Dulcie there, but his wife died two weeks later. Smith was very active at Battle being, among other things, its first medical officer of health. In 1881/82 he moved to St Leonards, where he married again and where he remained for the rest of his life. His sister married his successor as Battle medical officer of health.

At Battle he travelled on horseback to his more distant patients, keeping three horses at the Chequers Inn close to his house, one of which was always saddled ready for an emergency. When Sheila came to write books (the first published as early as 1907) she appears to have learned much of rural Sussex from accompanying him on his visits. In the 1911 census, when she was 24, she is listed as an author. Like so many writers, having begun early she carried on for the rest of her life.

When people move they often lose contact with earlier places of residence but this was not the case for the Smiths. Their house in Dane Road, St Leonards was named Battle Lodge. Sheila 'came out' at Battle:

That year saw me "come out" at the local Hunt Ball.... I stood hopefully at the Drill Hall at Battle, expecting the very best of life and mankind, and wearing a cream lace dress, forget-me-nots and galoshes. The last were an oversight and belonged to the rigours of a two hours' cab drive in January. The lace dress was, I think, quite pretty in itself, though it did not suit me, and I was far too pale to wear forget-me-nots.

I enjoyed the dance, but I did not care for those other aspects of social life to which it was portal.*

A notorious event occurred in April 1913 when suffragettes burned down the home of the former local MP. This was Levetleigh, opposite the Kaye-Smith house, which was owned by Harvey Du Cros, a stout opponent of Votes for Women; the action was part of the campaign for women's suffrage. Sheila described how, as a female author assumed to support them, she was accused of having set fire to the house: 'the evidence was clear – I had sat at the window, mocking the efforts of firefighters and shouting "Votes for Women"'. The accusations subsided only after the intervention of her father, who was most indignant that his daughter should have been accused. Sheila said that she slept through the event, only hearing of it when she awoke the next day. She must have indeed slept well, for local newspaper reports described the scene as very busy and noisy. It seems hard to believe that she could have avoided hearing anything.

She kept many connections in Battle, mainly with her father's old friends and their families. In the cemetery one can find the graves of her father, both his wives and Sheila's two sisters who had survived infancy. Sheila was a mover behind the Battle Pageant of 1932, involving nearly three thousand performers. The Sussex Agricultural Express described the event:

'a triumph for all connected with its organisation and presentation', taking place in the grounds of Battle Abbey, 'one of the most wonderful settings that can be imagined'.

It ran from 4 to 16 July with performances each evening and matinées twice a week. Sheila wrote the prologue, described by the

* All the quotations in this piece are by kind permission of Sheena Wenham.

press as 'highly effective'. It was delivered in a Sussex dialect (so favoured by Sheila in her writing) by Albert Richardson of Burwash, better known at the time as the wireless and gramophone artist Buttercup Joe. He delivered the prologue in a shepherd's smock while holding a crook, standing with a sheep dog beside a flock of sheep. At the end of the prologue he moved to the side of the arena where he went to sleep, to dream the events of the last 900 years, re-awakening at the end of the pageant. It was described as a 'simple scene but most effectively carried out'. Sheila became a vice-president of the Historical Society after its foundation in 1950.

Wills cigarette card: Famous British Authors, No 18,
Shaun Cooper, *The Shining Cord of Sheila Kaye-Smith*

In addition to her numerous novels, published almost annually between 1908 and 1956, she wrote a topography Weald of Kent and Sussex (1953). Her books include works on other authors, including John Galsworthy and Jane Austen. There were also three works of autobiography and two semi-autobiographical children's novels. She also wrote on a religious theme as well as poems and short stories.

She married Theodore Penrose Fry, an Anglican priest so near to Roman Catholicism that he found it hard to find a parish. In the end he did become a Catholic, taking Sheila with him. They bought land at Northiam, lived in an old oast that they converted to a house and built a local Catholic parish church where in the end she was to be buried.

St Theresa of Lisieux Church. © Copyright Tim Knight.

Her early novels were of the type parodied in *Cold Comfort Farm* by Stella Gibbons, but as she became more popular her style developed. Her later novels reflect her pre-occupation with her faith. All her novels were (and continue to be) of great local interest.

> There was never a time when I did not know and love the countryside outside Hastings – Platnix and the primrose lane by Ireland Farm, where father used to drive us as tiny children to fill our hands with flowers.

She did much to record the local Sussex dialect and accent, now almost lost. An example found in Sussex Gorse is typical:

> "I've found a way of gitting rid of them rootses – thought of it while I were working at the trees. I'm going the blast 'em out.
> "Blast 'em!"
> "Yes. Blast 'em wud gunpowder. I've heard of its being done. I'd never dig all the stuff out myself – yards of it there be – willer rootses always wur hemmed spready."
> "Its never bin done in these parts"
> "Well, it'll be done now, surelye".*

---

* If people wonder why Ardingly, for example, has its pronunciation the answer is above.

Her novel *Joanna Godden* (1921) has been identified as her most popular, being made into a film in 1947 starring Googie Withers, while *The end of the House of Alard* (1923), based on the history of a genuine Winchelsea family, sold most copies.

Her non-fiction works show a different side of Sheila – more reflective, revealing her wealth of knowledge and an intelligent, while very readable, style of writing. Her autobiographies are written in a particularly interesting way. *Three Ways Home* (1937) takes as its theme three strands of her life – the countryside of Kent and Sussex, her writing and her religious views, culminating together in her conversion to Catholicism. She provides details of her life as well as constructive comments and interesting insights into on her literary works, for example of *The Challenge to Sirius* (1917) she writes:

> It is a long, nervous, chaotic book, aiming at the sky but seldom hitting anything higher than a tree.

while of the publication of *The Tramping Methodist* (1908) she reveals that:

> The publisher wanted to see me, and an appointment was duly made; but my pleasure and excitement were a little dashed when I found that my parents absolutely refused to let me go to his office unchaperoned.

In *All the Books of my Life,* published posthumously, Sheila writes about books that she enjoyed, starting from her childhood favourites such as *Black Beauty* and *Alice in Wonderland*, through to the works of Agatha Christie, Conan Doyle and P G Wodehouse as well as those of Freud and Jung. Along the way she presents further autobiographical anecdotes, providing a yet fuller account of her life, including the revelation that she believed in predictive dreams, had an interest in extra-sensory perception and what she terms psychical research – perhaps surprising in a devout Catholic. She was far from being only a novelist.

The lucky historical writer

❧

Hesketh Pearson
(1887–1964)

Hesketh Pearson was another prolific author, if at first rather fortunate. He had 38 books published from 1921 until after the end of his life, when another followed. They were almost entirely on historical subjects, and some cases about people he had personally known.

Pearson had been born in rural Worcestershire in 1887, to a middle-class family that soon moved to Bedford. They were well-connected and claimed descent from Erasmus Darwin, grandfather of the more famous Charles, and Pearson's great-great-uncle was Sir Francis Galton, the champion of eugenics and, rather longer-lasting, the perfecter of fingerprint identification.

After Cambridge and various failures in the commercial world, by 1911 he was in London under the erratic patronage of Sir Herbert Beerbohm Tree and describing himself in the census as an actor. In 1912 he married another actor, Gladys Bardili (stage name Gladys Gardner) and they were together until her death in 1951, despite his persistent and often successful pursuit of other women. (Very shortly after Gladys died he rather quickly married their neighbour Joyce Ryder, who was to outlive him). One child was born to his first marriage, in 1913: Henry, who would join the International Brigade in the Spanish Civil War and would die from wounds received at the battle of the Ebro.

Pearson joined up in 1914 but was diagnosed as suffering from tuberculosis and discharged; a second attempt in the following year had the same result. He continued acting until 1916, when he managed finally to join the Army Service Corps as a Private (Driver). In 1917, with influential patronage from a royal, he was commissioned and sent to Mesopotamia where he suffered repeated illnesses. (He was sent to find a roadworthy route from there through Iran to the Caspian Sea in preparation for the British expedition to Baku.) His final rank was Captain, and he was awarded the Military Cross which, true to form, he always refused to mention, even in his memoirs. After his third discharge he returned to acting. His brother Jack was a founder and sub-editor of the *Wipers Times*; he also won the MC but reached the higher rank of Lieutenant Colonel.

Pearson's early literary career seemed unremarkable. During the war he had contributed to British newspapers and then he wrote two books about his experiences but was brought near to bankruptcy by his *Modern men and mummers*, which described in humorous but often negative terms most of the men whom he knew. He was saved by payments by Horatio Bottomley of all people. (After all, Pearson also championed Frank Harris, though Bottomley was a man of worse character.)

In 1926/27 notoriety found him. He had convinced Allen Lane of The Bodley Head (later to be founder of Penguin Books) that his book *The Whispering Gallery* was composed of entries from a diary of a senior diplomat. Pearson claimed that this was Sir Rennell Rodd, a Foreign Office grandee and, until shortly before then, the ambassador to Italy from 1908 to 1919, including the whole of the First World War; he had already published his own memoirs. On the basis of this story, Pearson obtained a cheque of £250 – or £225; accounts vary – in advance of royalties, which he returned before charges were laid against him. On publication, The *Daily Mail* (and then others) exposed him as a hoaxer. In the case of the *Mail* it was because its founder Lord Northcliffe (dead, but his brother owned the paper) came badly out of the book. Others simply could not believe that a senior diplomat would hold the views attributed to him or, even more so, write in the way that it was claimed.

Not unnaturally, Lane was annoyed; and the fact that money had changed hands exposed Pearson to a charge of obtaining it by false pretences. He was so charged in November 1926 and came up for trial in the following January. He rejected all appeals from family and friends to plead guilty. The trial was very brief but well-serviced: the prosecutor was Sir Henry Curtis-Bennett and the defence

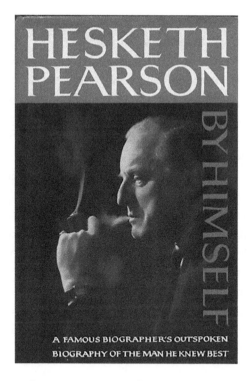

HESKETH
PEARSON

BY HIMSELF

A FAMOUS BIOGRAPHER'S OUTSPOKEN
BIOGRAPHY OF THE MAN HE KNEW BEST

barrister Sir Patrick Hastings, two of the best-known King's Counsel in England. Even Curtis-Bennett, however, could not prove intent to deceive, though he put both Rodd and Lane into the witness box. Pearson's defence was that the book was an obvious hoax and that he had returned the money before any threat of prosecution had been made. The jury acquitted him, much to the annoyance not only of Rodd but also of *The Times*, where the verdict prompted a very negative editorial. Rodd's letter of complaint appeared on the same day.

Understandably he suffered in the short run, not least because his public reputation might have deterred purchasers from any future work. He returned to the stage. Very shortly, however, he abandoned acting to concentrate on writing, and his notoriety proved short-lived. Penguin under Allen Lane published several of his later books. Pearson seemed to know everyone in the literary world, from Shaw, Belloc and Chesterton to the infamous Frank Harris, whom he championed if only to be provocative. He was a close friend of Hugh Kingsmill.

Pearson's connection with Sussex was due to the danger of living in London during the Second World War. To escape the blitz he moved to Woods Place at Whatlington in 1941, the next house along an unmade lane where Malcolm Muggeridge was already established but absent on war duty. Like Muggeridge, he was one of the most devoted customers of The Royal Oak as well as of several other pubs. Pearson – a serial adulterer – had an affair with Kitty Muggeridge while Muggeridge was in America. Admitted by Kitty later, it didn't bring to an end the men's friendship and collaboration. He moved back to London in 1945.

It took time for Pearson to develop a style and a theme, and it was serious biography, beginning with his ancestor Erasmus Darwin. Gladys helped with the research for her husband's books but by 1950 it was clear that she was no longer in a condition to do so and Pearson was on his own. His books still sell.

After Pearson's death Muggeridge wrote of his approach to religion as being similar to that of his subject, the Rev. Sydney Smith – the 'Smith of Smiths':

> They suited one another perfectly, and I trust that by this time they have met and compared notes in the celestial precincts reserved for Anglicans who in the days of their mortality were given to laying up treasure on earth, and regarding the Ten Commandments as like an examination paper, with seven only to be attempted.

Writer, broadcaster and sermoniser

⚜

Malcolm Muggeridge
(1903–90)

Muggeridge was a journalist, author, broadcaster and campaigner whose face and manner of speaking were instantly recognisable across Britain. He lived at the Mill House at Whatlington for some twenty years then moving to Park Cottage outside Robertsbridge, but he returned to be buried in Whatlington churchyard.

While in Sussex he had close relationships with the writers Hugh Kingsmill (at Hastings) and Hesketh Pearson, who lived for most of the Second Would War at Whatlington.

Muggeridge's journey through life was not unproblematic. His father had been a Labour MP and he was brought up on the Left. In his youth he was an admirer of Stalin's Russia, but that fell away with his personal knowledge of the famine of 1932, let alone of the later show trials.

In the early thirties there was much support for the Soviet Union among the British intelligentsia, including for example Bernard Shaw and Sidney and Beatrice Webb (and Muggeridge's wife Kitty was a niece both of Beatrice Webb and Stafford Cripps, another prominent left-winger). While this support drained away from most people and very quickly from Muggeridge, the rise of fascism and the breakdown of capitalism in 1929–32 lent it continued strength up to and including the Second World War.

After Cambridge, he was at first a teacher in India, Britain and Egypt, then a journalist on the *Manchester Guardian* (*MG*) – on Arthur Ransome's recommendation (he had, significantly or

Malcolm Muggeridge

otherwise, married Trotsky's secretary). It was for the *MG* that he went to Moscow in 1932, reporting back on the terrible scenes in Ukraine, reports of which, in the light of how Stalin was then viewed, were incompletely published. The independent Ukraine was to make him the posthumous award of the Order of Freedom in gratitude for his attempts to bring the Moscow-directed famine to general notice.

The argument over publication added to the tensions between Muggeridge and the new editor of the *MG*, and he left the paper. Thereafter he was mainly freelance.

This complicated man was of course far more than a scribbler. He joined up in 1939 thoroughly disillusioned with British politics and its unreadiness for war, by which time he had perfected the style that he displayed for the rest of his life: *The Thirties* is direct, witty, cynical and well-informed. In the war he served in intelligence, at first in Mozambique, which as a Portuguese colony was neutral, with diplomatic representation from all the warring powers.

He was a success and was later moved to the USA and Algeria and then, at the liberation, to Paris. There he was an early investigator of the case against PG Wodehouse, who had been caught in France by the Axis invasion. Imprisoned by the Germans and later subjected to house arrest, he made five light-hearted broadcasts to Britain on German radio. For these he was vilified by the British press that labelled him a collaborator. In the end no proceedings were taken against him, presumably on Muggeridge's recommendation.

Muggeridge and Wodehouse became friends as a result of their encounter. Wodehouse wrote in a letter: "I'm so glad that you like Malcolm Muggeridge. Words can't tell what a friend he has been to us." Muggeridge ended the war as a Major, awarded the French Croix de Guerre.

He returned to journalism, becoming a deputy editor of The *Daily Telegraph*, and edged into broadcasting at a time when the BBC – the only broadcasting organisation – was still beset by deference to the great and the good and by something more than that to the royal family. His work there was controversial for the time but it helped lead the way to a much more open and popular kind of interviewing. His wit and humour must have helped him when editor of *Punch* in the fifties (and as guest editor of *Private Eye* in the sixties); he was a sharp interviewer and commentator.

Muggeridge was a compulsive writer, and the titles of his books show his political and spiritual journey. The early ones tend to be historical, and there are memoirs, but from the sixties the mood changed with the publication of *Jesus Rediscovered*. Thereafter there were several books about Christianity, including sermons. He fell out with modern Britain, becoming ever more strident in his denunciation of pop culture and overt sexuality, drug use, contraception and all the characteristics that were then newly open.

He joined vigorously in campaigns against what he saw as a civilisation losing its values and moving towards dissolution, primarily sexual dissolution. He was far from alone in that: his co-warriors Lord Longford and Mary Whitehouse were also well-known. In 1979 he attacked Monty Python's film *Life of Brian* in a television discussion with its creators, but had to admit that he had not actually seen it. His severance from mass culture was now complete. This cannot have dismayed him, for he found the masses unattractive, just as he found politicians and others with power interested only in retaining it. This cynicism was consistent with his religious belief.

His BBC interview with the then unknown Mother Teresa in 1967 brought her to wide notice in the West and his regard for her and her faith may have been a factor in his and Kitty's decision in 1982 to convert to Roman Catholicism. Indeed, apart from memoirs all his late works were associated with his Christian beliefs.

Muggeridge continued to write, though less prolifically, and was clearly in retirement. He declared that he had always felt like a stranger in a strange world, and perhaps it was this sense of detachment that made him unique among mid-century commentators. He wrote that he had never been able to take seriously any form of authority, though presumably he could embrace the authority of Pope John Paul II. He was a wonderful writer: informed, thoughtful, witty – and certainly provocative. On the other side of the coin he has recently been outed as an enthusiastic adulterer and serial groper of women during his time at the BBC. Unfortunately, as we know, he was far from alone in this.

He was to die having been a vigorous and conservative Roman Catholic. He was not the only one to make this conversion; perhaps the need for a faith of some kind is fundamental to many even if, in Muggeridge's case, he spent most of his life as a professed agnostic. Age took its toll of him, and towards the end he had to live in care homes, at Loose Farm at Battle then at Bexhill. He died at home at Robertsbridge. Kitty, herself a remarkable character, is buried with him at Whatlington. She had five children with him.

Writer of history and travel

⨷

Averil Mackenzie-Grieve
(1903–83)

Mackenzie-Grieve was born at Rotherfield and died at Robertsbridge. Her family would have been better-off had her father not lost money in Argentina but it remained comfortable. Averil was brought up mainly in Devon. She had a good voice and there are press reports of her singing solo at various events.

She had an interesting and very well-travelled life, not without its tragedy. Though she wrote well and was well-informed her name is little-known now. Her books are mainly historical:

Sacrifice to Mars
The Last Years of the English Slave Trade
The Waterfall
Clara Novello
Aspects of Elba

A Gibbet for Myself
The Brood of Time
The Great Accomplishment
A Race of Green Ginger
Time and Chance

For *The Brood of Time*, C P Snow wrote in *T* in 1949: "a remarkable work of art … received both for its nostalgia and its insight". Another reviewer wrote that "the author shows moments of real skill".

She also published her translation of Camillo Spreti's *Description of the Island of Malta in 1764* and edited, with her own wood-engravings, *The New London Letter Writer 1794*.

In fact her first interest was wood-carving, though she was also an accomplished painter. These talents had been noticed at school, and she went on to become a full-time artist. By 1924 she was sufficiently well-known to provide four wood-cuts to illustrate the poem Tom o' Bedlam, and more before the Second World War. She spent some time in Italy, the first of her many visits outside the UK. Her life was full of travel.

She married Cyril le Gros Clark in 1935 (the work of his brother Wilfred, among his other achievements, would be crucial in the exposure of the Piltdown Man as a fraud). He had had a distinguished service in the First World War, being wounded in France and then, in the Indian Army, being among those who entered Jerusalem with General Allenby two years later. He joined the civil service of the British Protectorate of Sarawak and then spent three years in China studying its language, literature and history before returning to be Secretary for Chinese Affairs. In 1935, at the Rajah's invitation, he returned to Sarawak as Chief Secretary, taking Averil with him. At this point she seems to have generally given up wood-carving. She travelled around the East, just as when younger, she had travelled around other parts of Europe and would do so again after World War Two. For more than two years she was with her husband in China, where he was the Rajah's representative.

He was back in Sarawak before the Japanese invaded, though at that point Averil was in London. In July 1945 the Japanese took Cyril out of Batu Lintang internment camp and shot him at Keningau. Official lists after the war still included him but presumably out of a lack of confirmation.

She later married John Keevil, a naval doctor born in Brazil and awarded the DSO in the Second World War, and they moved to the attractive old George Hill House at Robertsbridge. He was Keeper of the Library of the Royal College of Physicians and a distinguished author in his own right on topics of medical history and biography. He died at hospital in Hastings in 1976. She was to die at home at Robertsbridge.

The Home Front chronicler

❦

Elizabeth Jane Howard
(1923–2014)

At least one commentator suggests that Howard would have been a better writer had she not been engaged in three marriages and various affairs. But she was still very good.

She spent much of her formative years at her grandparents' houses near Battle, first at Home Place in Whatlington, then at The Beacon near Staplecross. She used Home Place as the setting for her best-selling *The Cazalet Chronicles*, a five-novel family saga spanning the period before, during, and after the Second World War. Battle, its station, shops, and surroundings, is highly recognisable; Howard was meticulously accurate in the details of her settings. This accuracy contributes to the charm and readability of her novels. Her readers feel drawn into a real place, inhabited by real people.

Howard's grandfather – "the Brig" in the novels – ran the family timber business. He renovated his Sussex houses using fine quality panelling and floors made of jarrah wood, a rare wood from Western Australia; some of these interiors survive. The family was comfortably off and traditional in its attitudes. Sons joined the family firm, daughters were educated mainly at home, by governesses. Jane, as Elizabeth Jane Howard was always known, lived in London with her father David, who was charming but "duplicitous and unsafe", and her mother Kit, daughter of the composer Sir Arthur Somervell.

Kit had given up a career with Diaghilev's *Ballets Russes* for an ultimately unhappy marriage to the philandering David. Jane, acutely aware of tensions which she would later examine in her fiction, took refuge in the warm, relaxed atmosphere of the extended family life in Sussex. "I spent the mornings up apple trees reading Captain Marryat

Elizabeth Jane Howard
Courtesy of BBC News at bbc.co.uk/news.

and R.M. Ballantyne", she recalled. She explored the countryside, which she loved deeply, in company with her cousins.

A university place for the highly intelligent but sketchily educated Jane was not considered. She took cooking and secretarial courses, did some modelling, and spent a season acting in repertory in Devon; she played Kate to the young Paul Scofield's Petruchio in *The Taming of the Shrew*. These experiences, too, would be incorporated into her novels. Jane's striking beauty shaped her life. As one male employer put it, she was

> so beautiful that continuous problems arose ... Little in the way of completely normal business was possible or sensible when she was in the room.

In 1942, aged only 19, Jane made the first of three marriages. Her husband was Peter Scott, son of the doomed Polar explorer Robert Falcon Scott. Peter was in his thirties, a painter and ornithologist on active naval service. His powerful mother, the sculptor Kathleen Kennet, was very much the third person in the marriage; Jane brilliantly describes her influence in her novel *Confusion*. The marriage produced a daughter, Nicola, born during an air raid, who was to be Jane's only child. Jane and Peter separated in 1946, with Peter taking custody of Nicola.

Jane found herself alone and hard up, but at last free to explore her growing belief that she wanted to be a writer. Her first novel, *The Beautiful Visit*, was published in 1950. It was followed in 1956 by the critically-acclaimed *The Long View*. Male attention both helped and distracted her from her literary career. Her lovers included writers such as Laurie Lee, Cecil Day-Lewis and Arthur Koestler – the last refused to use contraception, but also refused any responsibility for the resulting pregnancy, which Jane decided to terminate, at a time when abortion was still illegal.

In 1958 there was a second, brief, marriage, to Jim Douglas-Henry, an Australian broadcaster and fellow writer. Then in 1965 Jane met Kingsley Amis while organising the Cheltenham Literary Festival. The couple moved to an elegant Georgian house in Barnet where Jane, an accomplished cook, entertained literary friends and did her best to be a good stepmother to Kingsley's three children. But life with the heavy-drinking novelist was not easy. Jane's writing took second place to Kingsley's. After eighteen turbulent years they divorced.

Jane did not marry again, but eventually retreated to Bungay, a Suffolk village, where she felt free to write and live life on her own terms. However, her lifelong desire to be loved was still alive, and led her, in old age, into the thrall of an emotional fraudster. She wrote about this experience with unflinching honesty in her 1998 book *Falling*.

Encouraged by her novelist stepson Martin Amis, in the 1990s Jane embarked on the *The Cazalet Chronicles: The Light Years, Marking Time, Confusion*, and *Casting Off*. (The fifth and final volume, *All Change*, appeared in 2013; it would be her last book.) The novels were highly successful, and have been dramatised for television and radio. The Cazalets, based on the real-life Howards, are prosperous members of the English upper middle class who find themselves making huge adjustments as the Nazi threat becomes a reality. Other people's stories – friends, servants, lovers – are interwoven; a particularly memorable character is the elderly family governess Miss

Milliment, who buried all hope of romance when her young man was killed in the First World War. Indeed, Howard is especially skilful at showing how the trauma of the first war has shaped the emotions and attitudes of its survivors, who now face a second global conflict.

Howard set the novels at Home Place, but combined her memories of it with elements of The Beacon – for instance the Babies' Hotel, the charity run by selfless Aunt Rachel, is based on a real-life enterprise housed in the converted barn and squash courts at The Beacon. Plenty of action takes place elsewhere, most notably in Blitz-torn London, but the Battle area lies at the heart of the *Chronicles*. Howard's evocation of period detail – food, clothes, transport – is flawless, and combines with her sympathetic delineation of character and skilful plotting to make these novels one of the most enjoyable ways of finding out about life in and around Battle during this fascinating period.

3
Artists

This is not a complete set: it might have been possible to include among the artists James Inskipp (c. 1792–1868) of Battle, Edward Patry (1856–1940) of Sedlescombe or Cecil Bacon (1905–92) of Battle.

England's greatest gardener

✥

Lancelot 'Capability' Brown
(c. 1716–83)

Brown was Britain's greatest landscape gardener and his work is impressively shown at Ashburnham Place close to Battle. He was involved there for about 15 years, from the mid-1760s. He made a lasting contribution to the landscape of Sussex.

Brown changed the face of many eighteenth-century English estates, moving hills, creating new lakes and serpentine rivers, all within naturalistic parkland with rolling grass and selective retention of existing woodland copses plus new tree plantings – particularly of cedar of Lebanon, his signature tree. He was not just a landscape architect but also designed houses, churches, follies and garden structures. He was renowned for his skill in engineering large water features.

Once his career took off his work quickly became highly fashionable and a huge amount of work came his way. He was a constant traveller and workaholic and is reckoned to have designed 265 landscapes in England, of which 170 survive. Among them are the well-known gardens of Stowe in Buckinghamshire, Chatsworth in Derbyshire and Alnwick Castle in Northumberland.

Yet his background was very ordinary. He must have owed much to the promise he showed as an imaginative early gardener, impressing his co-workers and landlords alike. Among the former was William Kent, another well-known landscape designer (and later to be his father-in-law). It is said that Brown owed his nickname Capability by his judgment on lands shown to him – that there was 'capability' of improvement.

Brown was born at Kirkhale in Northumberland where his father was land agent to the landowner, his mother being a chambermaid.

He was a gardener there before moving on, presumably being recommended by the landlord or by Kent, to Boston and then to Stowe. There he became Kent's assistant.

The usual English garden fashion was an imitation of the French, being much impressed by the geometric formality of Versailles, and Kent was an early mover away towards a more rural style. Brown followed him and developed it further, being responsible for the remarkable Grecian valley at Stowe that has two of his trademarks, flowing water and a classical building. He emphasised changing views, wherever one went on or by an estate. He saw buildings as an integral part of the landscape, not simply as unrelated to their surroundings. Water was not just there, occasionally flooding the park, but it was to be trapped into lakes and to fall in cascades.

The National Trust currently looks after 18 gardens by Brown, though Ashburnham Place is not one of them. There he dammed the stream in front of the house and named it Broad Water; he also designed the Orangery.

Brown became involved with the second Earl of Ashburnham before 1767. One of the positions the earl held at court in 1753-62 was

Ashburnham Place: the terrace and lake in front of the house created by Capability Brown.

Capability Brown,
Modified extract from a Sun Insurance advertisement, 1964

Keeper of Hyde and St James's Parks, which he relinquished only two years before Brown's appointment as Royal Gardener for Hampton Court and St James's. He knew Brown's work and indeed in 1758 had signed a petition that he given an appointment at Kensington Gardens.

The precise date of Brown's first tasks at Ashburnham isn't clear. He produced a large detailed plan of about 1.27 by 1.91m dimensions (over 4' by 5' 3"). It showed the land to the north and south of the house all as parkland, a chain of three lakes and woodland south of them, and further afield more open land rising towards the ridge leading to Netherfield. It also showed an intended walled garden. Among other proposals were a bridge, new stables, an icehouse and menagerie. There was also a network of drives, for then the local estate extended to around 3,237ha of which 90 ha (about 8,000 and 220 acres) were gardens and pleasure grounds around the house and church.

It was before 1767 that he received a first payment, dutifully recorded in his accounts book. His account was settled with the earl in 1773, but it was re-opened a year later with a final payment in 1781. He directly received £7,196 1s 0d. But overall a minimum of £16,203 4s 3d was paid, including Brown's fees, to Brown's son-in-law the architect Henry Holland, to the decorative painter John Wateridge and to the foreman Jonathan Midgeley. This would represent about £3M at 2020 prices.

The house had several revisions in the years to come but the park landscape overall remains a relatively unaltered example of Brown's work.

It is possible that Brown was responsible for improvements to the grounds of Battle Abbey, for example in containing the stream in ponds and arranging the trees. There is no proof of this but the changes are very much in his style.

Other places in Sussex where Brown worked were further away, mostly towards the western boundary of the county, but nearer home were Compton Place at Eastbourne and Sheffield Park. It may be that he advised the Fullers of Brightling but if so they appear to have taken no notice.

Architect and vicar, at home and in New Zealand

Frederick Thatcher
(1814–1890)

In Britain we know Thatcher as an architect only for the Battle workhouse, opened in 1840. He is much better known in New Zealand. The attractively-fronted workhouse was not just for

The old workhouse as housing today,
courtesy of Bev Marks

Battle, for it was the poor-law centre for fifteen parishes. It was designed for 440 inmates and looked different from the conventional constructions that resembled gloomy tenements, though its rear is in fact typical of those. It was Gothic in style with some hints of Tudor times; it must have conformed to the principles set out in the model plans circulated by the Poor Law Commission.

Quite how Thatcher landed this major contract is unclear. He was a Hastings man, born in the Old Town to a family long there; his mother 'owned some land'. He became one of the first 15 associates of the new Institute of British Architects in London (now the Royal Institute of British Architects), being admitted in 1836.

It may be significant that one of its founders in 1834 was Decimus Burton of St Leonards-on-Sea fame, of which he designed much after 1828. We have no information about where or when Thatcher decided that architecture was his career path, though we might guess that he was influenced by Burton.

He ceased working as an architect in Britain in 1843 and was taken by the Himalaya to New Plymouth on the west coast of North Island, New Zealand. We don't know why, other than that his first wife had just died and maybe demand for his architecture had stalled.

By 1843 New Zealand badly needed European immigrants. Three years earlier, when the treaty of Waitangi had allowed the UK to declare it a colony, their population had been only about 2000. The small number meant that few were likely to specialise in particular occupations and Thatcher was no exception. He began by farming in the area but soon moved to Auckland – perhaps because of major arguments over land ownership in the area of New Plymouth - where his skills as an architect were noticed and put to good use, particularly in church building by Bishop George Augustus Selwyn, who appears later in this account. Thatcher then worked as a land auctioneer, as superintendent of public works (1845–46), lieutenant in the Auckland Militia (1845), and assistant private secretary to the Governor (1846–48). He designed Auckland's Anglican minister-training St John's College's chapel, consecrated in 1847, and he became also the college's bursar and auditor.

By then he felt the call of religion and was ordained priest at St John's in 1853. He became of perhaps even greater use to the Church by designing more churches, almost entirely of wood, the natural local building material.

He married again, his first wife having died shortly before he left Britain, and his wife had a son. But Thatcher was not well. He developed a throat problem and in 1856, with the family, he returned to England. We don't know what he did there before resuming his

New Zealand interests five years later as vicar of St Paul's, Wellington, which he built from native New Zealand wood and which is now preserved. But after it was completed his illness recurred and the family went back home for the last time.

Back in England he called on George Selwyn, by then Bishop of Lichfield. He became Selwyn's chaplain and a prebendary canon of the cathedral. He became one of the main proponents of a Cambridge college in the name of Selwyn, who had died in 1878; it opened in 1882. He was a member of the College Council until his death. There is a memorial to him in Lincoln Cathedral.

The interior of Old St Paul's, Wellington,

The landlord painter

❧❦

Hercules Brabazon Brabazon
(1821–1906)

Brabazon owed his repetitive name to his inheritance. He was born Hercules Brabazon Sharpe but had inherited large Irish estates from his mother's family provided that he took their surname. He was also to inherit Oaklands, in Sedlescombe, from his father.

Born in Paris, he was educated at Harrow and Cambridge, after which he moved on to law; but a life in the courts did not appeal to him. Rome was calling, with its artistic heritage; and back in England he made other contacts useful to a largely self-taught painter.

As an adult he spent much of his time abroad but was at home for most of the various censuses. He lived mainly at Westminster, where he was a magistrate. He would die at Oaklands, leaving the comfortable sum of £39,271 8s 6d. He had leased Oaklands to the Combe family, who had married into his.

Brabazon specialised in watercolours, in a sub-Turner style. He travelled widely, including the Middle East, India and Africa. He was prolific, producing thousands of works, including water-colours of Athens, Capri, Delhi, Cairo, Algiers, Geneva, Amiens and Venice. He was no loner, however, counting among his friends many of the literary and artistic circles of the time. Having sufficient wealth and in the style of his class not given to boasting, Brabazon had to be persuaded to exhibit his pictures but once he did they became popular.

A gallery of his work opened posthumously at Sedlescombe in 1910 but as with so many others the Combe family was to fall on harder times. In 1926 they sold their collection of his paintings, no doubt hoping for a renewal of their wealth, but times had changed.

Unwisely they sold them all at once: three sales in just over two years, and 3,200 works. Predictably they fetched only small if not derisory sums. Prices were as low as £1 per drawing; they would do much better now.

Landscape with Industrial Buildings by a River, c. 1890

Coast Scene (believed to be Mont St Michel)

The sculptor friend of
Lenin and Trotsky

❦

Clare Sheridan
(1885–1970)

orn Clare Consuelo Frewen at Brede Place, Sheridan was a
remarkable sculptress whose career led to all kinds of so far
unsubstantiated stories of her personal life. The popular press
of the twentieth century revelled in such lubricious speculation, as it
does today, particularly where the subject is so obviously attractive
and well-connected.

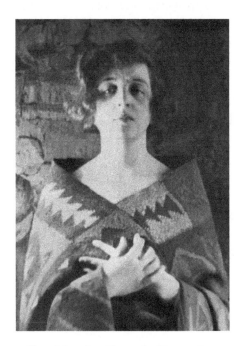

Clare Frewen Sheridan by Francis Bruguiere, c. 1922

Her father Moreton Frewen (1853–1924),* was a financial failure but was personally highly regarded and a friend of literary and political figures; her mother was an American, Clara Jerome, the aunt of Winston Churchill and by no means short of money. Young Clare was introduced to a large number of wealthy, literary and political people. She had a conventional education for her class, being sent to France and Germany, but a rebellious streak was evident.

In 1910, initially against the wishes of her parents she married a stockbroker, Wilfred Sheridan (who called himself William), a descendant of the playwright, Richard Brinsley Sheridan. In her marriage vows she declined to 'obey'. The couple had three children, Elizabeth, who died as an infant, Margaret, born in 1912, and Richard, born only a few days before Wilfred was killed in action on the Western Front. She was going to marry a nobleman but he too was killed in action. She never re-married, though from time to time the newspapers reported on the possibility.

In 1914, prompted by the widow of the painter G F Watts, Mary Fraser-Tytler, she sculpted the figure of a weeping angel for the grave of her daughter Elizabeth. She was then sufficiently motivated to develop her talent as a sculptress, studying the art and practice of sculpture, learning from Jacob Epstein among others. Very shortly she became well-known. Within four years she was holding exhibitions, and by 1917 her specialism – busts of well-known people – was attracting much attention, leading to work and the opportunity to portray world figures.

When the war ended the October Revolution had taken place in Russia. The first Soviet trade delegation arrived in the UK in 1920, led by Lev Kamenev, and it was understandable that the Bolsheviks would want their leaders commemorated in sculpture. Clare may have had an affair with Kamenev, who like so many of his comrades was destined to end up being shot on Stalin's orders.

Her brother Oswald wrote:

[She] is trying to go to Moscow with Kamenev to sculpt Lenin and Leon Trotsky.... I rather she didn't go but she has got Bolshevism badly - she always reflects the views of the last man she's met – and

___

* See Chapter 11

I think it may cure her to go and see it. She is her own mistress and if I thwarted her by telling Winston, she'd never confide in me again.... I went to the Bolshevik Legation in Bond Street with her and waited while she saw Kamenev. Several typical Bolshies there - degenerate lot.

Sheridan made a bust of Kamenev and went on holiday with him to the Isle of Wight. He took her to Russia in September 1920 where she produced busts of twelve people.

Clare Sheridan (*left*) in her London studio with busts of (*from left*) Zinoviev, Trotsky, Lenin and Dzerzhinsky (from *The Times*, 25 November 1920, image improved by Peter Greene**).**
The bust behind her does not appear to be part of the Soviet group. Lenin died in 1924; Dzerzhinsky founded the Soviet secret police and died, apparently from natural causes, in 1926; Zinoviev was executed on the same day as Kamenev in 1936; Trotsky was exiled, then murdered on Stalin's orders in 1940.

When she arrived in Russia the British were ensconced in the far north of the country in an ultimately unpursued campaign to unseat the Bolsheviks, and her cousin Churchill happened to be Secretary of State for War. He among others was hardly amused at his cousin's closeness to his enemies. It did not help that although not herself a Communist she was known then, as Oswald pointed out, to harbour strong sympathies with the Soviet régime.

She lived for two months in or close to the Kremlin at Moscow.

I was given comfortable quarters in a requisitioned house. Both Lenin and Trotsky are excellent sitters. I had eight hours with Lenin and 20 with Trotsky. Trotsky talked pictures, art and literature. He had the head of a Mephisto. He had a wonderful personality and is full of fire. He has read the best English literature, and once said to me that if England had never done anything but produce Shakespeare she would have justified her existence.

More rumours of affairs abounded, including one with Trotsky. He invited her to go with him to the front (the civil war was still on) but winter approached and she wanted to return to see her children. She left Moscow late in 1920, bringing back the model busts for casting in bronze; Russia had the copyright and she would send the final versions there.

Of Lenin she said:

From the art point of view I think he is the most interesting man in the world. His eyes are most extraordinary. I modelled him in his room at the War Office while he was at work at his desk. His calmness in all circumstances is extraordinary. No matter how excited others get he always preserves his impassiveness.

Her talks with the Bolshevik leaders formed the basis of a series of articles she wrote for *The Times*. Some people retained a suspicion that she was a Soviet spy but by that time her enthusiasm for the Soviet leaders – and theirs for her – had begun to wane. Clearly she was no communist, and her close ties with Churchill were unlikely to endear her to the USSR. They refused her any further contacts until 1924 when the Soviet representative in London let her go to Ukraine to see how much better things were than when she had last been in the country.

She and Oswald climbed on to a motorbike *Satanella* and drove off across Europe. He claimed that the only way she obtained a visa was because "Rakovsky's* fallen for her. They all do. And in the end she'll be shot." But they both survived, and Clare obtained sufficient material for a later book.

She had already become a journalist, at first for a North American

---

* Christian Rakovsky was president of Ukraine and would end up being shot on Stalin's orders in 1941.

publication, and had travelled around Europe covering various matters such as the Irish civil war (being one of the last to interview Michael Collins, who apologised to her for his men having burned down the family house in County Cork, where Clare had occasionally lived) and the Turco-Greek war including the appalling fate of Smyrna in September 1922. She interviewed several notable people such as Kemal Atatürk, the tsar of Bulgaria and Benito Mussolini. The last was not an occasion when he made a conquest, though it's hard to believe that he didn't attempt one. He threatened to send his fascist police after her if she published anything – a foolish threat because without punishment she soon wrote:

> Mussolini is a striking example of force and feebleness. He can be completely controlled by those around him, and, unfortunately, his entourage contains no-one of any intellectual or moral value.

An early report was of a meeting addressed by Hitler, and as she travelled around there were interviews with Maxim Gorky and with Primo de Rivera, who had carried out a coup d'état in Spain. She reported on the conditions in Germany during the currency crisis of 1923, and went on to Poland then Turkey, Romania and Algeria.

She also went to the USA and had to deny rumours that she had married Charlie Chaplin. But she did do a little sculpting and created a bust of him.

By now we know that Clare was not one for sitting still. She went back to North America where she learned to carve wood. Clare's memorial to her son, Richard, can be found in the parish church at Brede and her carvings appear in other English churches.

When war started again she came home, living initially at Brede Place Cottage – Brede Place itself was occupied by a local solicitor – but then at Oranmore in County Galway in 1947–54, and later at the Spanish arch in Galway city. Returning to Sussex she lived at Belmont House on the slope of the East Hill at Hastings.

There she wrote a further book of reminiscences. In 1960 she became a Franciscan nun. It was at Parham House near Beaminster in Dorset that she died.

Her last exhibition had been in 1951. A list of her sculptures has not been compiled but it included many subjects other than those mentioned above, including Gandhi and Asquith (now in the Imperial War Museum) and the dancer Serge Lifar.

She wrote several books, most of them highly praised, based on her travel experiences, mainly in Russia and America.

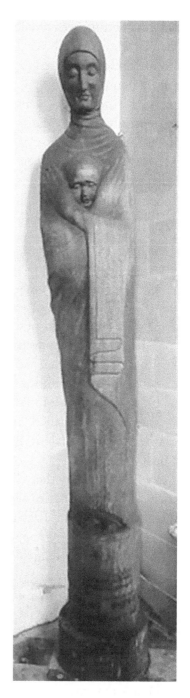

Madonna and child: Clare's memorial to her son Richard, in St George's church, Brede

A First World War artist

❧❧

Herbert Arnould Olivier

(1861–1952)

The Olivier family made quiet contributions to British life in the nineteenth century, moving to greater things in the twentieth: a major painter, a politician-cum-colonial governor and an internationally-acclaimed actor. Along the way they collected two peerages, now extinct.

Herbert was Battle's contribution to the family. His father Henry Arnold (*sic*) Olivier was Rector of Crowhurst in 1861–64. After school at Sherborne he determined on an artistic career and studied at the Royal Academy, winning the Creswick Prize there in 1882. From then on he exhibited and taught in various places and in 1917 became an official war artist. His war paintings are in the possession of the Imperial War Museum. His style was very much of the period. He was subject to early influence by the Pre-Raphaelites but soon moved on. His portraits are highly regarded, though his landscapes seem to have attracted less notice.*

Herbert gained his slightly odd middle name from his mother, born Anne Elizabeth Hardcastle Arnould. His male antecedents, descended from immigrant Huguenots, were almost always Anglican clergy and some moved around the country with some speed. His father had connections with the dioceses of the dioceses of Hereford, Salisbury, St Edmundsbury, St Albans and Winchester as well as with Chichester.

A brother, Sydney, achieved fame. His radicalisation began early: at Oxford he became a friend of Graham Wallas, who went on to

---

* A view of many of his pictures may be had through the website of the Imperial War Museum

**Portrait of Marshal Joffre, 9th February 1915, by
Herbert Arnould Olivier**

be one of the founders of the London School of Economics. This
brought him into contact with a wide variety of people. He was
sent abroad by the Colonial Office from time to time, notably as
Governor of Jamaica from 1907, and he became Secretary of State
for India in the first, very short, Labour government of 1924, when
he received a peerage. He was also a writer and playwright, generally
on radical topics.

Both these men were uncles to Laurence Olivier, whose popular
fame with us now rather eclipses them and who was to provide the
second and now-extinct peerage. Laurence was not local, having
been born in Surrey.

4
Entertainers and Actors

Stanley Holloway's
comic verse writer

❧

George Marriott Edgar
(1880–1951

Locally the best known of Edgar's verse is *The Battle of Hastings,* which ends:

> And after the battle were over
> They found 'Arold so stately and grand,
> Sitting there with an eye-full of arrow
> On his 'orse with his 'awk in his 'and.

Edgar was to live his last years at Battle. He is now little known, for the style in which his words came to the public no longer carries popularity. But in his day one could find people freely reciting his words not only in performances but in pubs and at home. They were a kind of community singing and made people laugh. Perhaps they didn't know they were his, because the public reciter was very often the well-known actor Stanley Holloway.

Edgar came from a Lancashire family that formed a theatre troupe. He was born in Kirkcudbright, no doubt on tour,. His parents had married in 1875, but neither was aware that his father had already had an illegitimate child by an actress. This boy turned out to be the celebrated author Edgar Wallace, and it was a long time before the connection became known: in fact the Kirkcudbright Edgar remained ignorant of it until he met Wallace in Hollywood not long before his death there. Edgar used the name Wallace for the lion (of *Albert and the Lion*), perhaps by coincidence.

Like the scions of so many theatrical families Edgar took to the

George Marriott Edgar in pantomime dame costume

stage, and began to come to notice in the long running *The co-optimists* in London in 1921–22. It was there that he met Holloway, who had already started his series of monologues. From 1930 Edgar supplied the words and their piano accompaniment.

Edgar wrote 30 monologues, including 16 for Holloway, and the scripts of 19 films for Gainsborough Pictures, 18 of them comedies. They included *Oh Mr Porter!* and *The Ghost Train*.

Edgar married in 1904, and he died at his house (Broom, North Trade Road, Battle). His wife died there ten years later.

A most popular actor

❧

Harry Andrews
(1911–89)

Two actors lie side by side in Salehurst churchyard: Harry Andrews and his partner Basil Hoskins. They had lived together in the village, and the Salehurst Halt pub displays a photograph of Andrews.

He was one of the most prominent British actors of the 1950–80 period, never retiring. Best known for his film and TV performances, like most such actors he began on the stage. This was at the Liverpool Playhouse in 1933, with his first London performance two years later. Like almost every other young man he was called up for military service, and at the end of the war resumed his theatrical career, including a stint with the Royal Shakespeare Company at Stratford in 1949–51. At various times he toured at Antwerp, New York and Brussels, and he was with the Royal Shakespeare in their tour of Australia.

Such a highly thought-of actor would be on film directors' wanted lists, and in 1953 he played the first of about 80 film roles, adding television rather later. Several films are seen today, through television, among them *Ice Cold in Alex* and *The Charge of the Light Brigade*. He was well-suited to playing soldiers, very much looking the part, and military films were then very popular. Sometimes he was less successful: while one can't always trust critics, one wrote of his Hamlet that his "well-spoken King looked like a futuristic cinema commissionaire".

He was tall, tough-looking and well-suited to the parts that he often played. He was the favourite of many women but for all his life it would have been unwise to reveal that he was gay. Fellow-actors were well aware of it and would not have been at all concerned, but his

Harry Andrews, 1970 by Allan Warren,

audiences might have reacted badly: after all, until 1967 homosexual practices among men were illegal and they remained controversial for some time afterwards. Basil Hoskins played very many fewer leading roles than Andrews, but he joined him in *Ice Cold*.

Andrews's films began as early as 1939, and his last was first shown in the year after his death. They included *Moby Dick* (1956), *Ice Cold in Alex* (1958), *Reach for Glory* (1962), *55 Days at Peking* (1963), *633 Squadron* (1964), *The Agony and the Ecstasy* (1965), *Battle of Britain* (1969), *Nicholas and Alexandra* (1971), *Man of La Mancha* (1972) and *The Four Feathers* (1978).

During much of this time he maintained the family home at Seaford, where his father had been a doctor, before buying the house at Salehurst.

The most popular bandleader
of his time

❧

Frank Chacksfield
(1914–95)

In the 1950s and early 1960s the Battle-born Chacksfield was one
of Britain's best-loved musical entertainers in Britain, but his style
fell sharply out of fashion.

His music was a mainstay of the BBC Light Programme – easy-
listening music played by a 40-piece orchestra that reflected but
also led the then popular musical fashions. Then they were at first
rivalled and fairly soon obliterated by the arrival of rock and other
styles from 1956 onwards. Chacksfield adjusted towards a smoother,
more contemplative kind of music. Today even that work would
be profoundly unfashionable: the sounds of his near-contemporary
Mantovani, for example, are reputed to clear a room. Nevertheless
Chacksfield continued to record until the 1990s.

He was a good pianist who started early, playing at local festivals
and being deputy organist at Salehurst parish church. Where Frank's
musical talent came from is unknown. He clearly had drive. Working
in a solicitor's office at Battle, with friends from Battle he formed his
first band in 1933/34: The Hastorians. At least one player left school
when Chacksfield recruited him, the drummer Bill Nash (son of a
fishmonger at 52 High Street and a close neighbour in Wellington
Gardens). Engagements came quickly, and soon the band had a
regular slot at Hilden Manor at Tonbridge. They continued playing
together until the war began, and kept in touch afterwards.

Frank turned professional in 1937. When the war came he joined
the Signals but during an illness showed his talent as a pianist and
was posted to ENSA. There he became a close colleague of the (now

The band at Hilden Manor,
courtesy of Georgina Doherty, Bill Nash's niece.

nearly forgotten) comic Charlie Chester and this gave him an entrée to the BBC after the war. Not only did he play but he also composed and conducted; his music won awards in the UK and elsewhere. He is celebrated in a display in Battle Museum.

Chacksfield married at Sedlescombe in 1946. The wedding was attended by show-business greats of the day including Charlie Chester and Arthur Haynes. There were no children.

At his end he merited a long obituary in *The Times*, recording his domination of light music that resulted, for example, in his capture of the American market in the early 1950s.

Frank Chacksfield and his orchestra made more than 150 long-playing albums over 25 years which were released in Japan, France, Germany and Australia and the United States as well as in Britain. His 35 albums for Decca alone are estimated to have achieved sales of more than 20 million.

The gifted Harold Steptoe

❦

Harry H Corbett
(1925–82)

Harry H Corbett

Many actors start well but then get typecast. Corbett was one of them. After an unpromising start in life he trained as an actor using the Method approach, and up to the early sixties was regarded as one of the most impressive up-and-coming classical actors.

Corbett was born in Rangoon, Burma, the youngest of seven children of an NCO in the South Staffordshire Regiment, a professional soldier who had survived two wounds and a gassing in the First World War. His mother died (of dysentery, common enough in Burma) when he was only 18 months old; he was sent to live with an aunt in Manchester, in the poor area of Ardwick. He passed the tests for entry to the local grammar school but his aunt couldn't afford the expense. Leaving school at 14, he had various jobs: greengrocer's errand boy, plumber's mate, plastics moulder, male nurse and car sprayer.

When he reached the right age in 1942, he joined the Royal Marines, serving first at Scapa Flow and in the Atlantic, and was part of the crew delivering the exiled Norwegian royal family back to Oslo in May 1945. Later that year he was in the Far East where he saw active service in New Guinea. He deserted at Tonga and went to Australia but gave himself up.

Back in civilian life he trained as a radiographer, but then decided to become an actor, at first in repertory in Manchester and then with the Theatre Workshop at Stratford East. This was a highly-regarded nursery of promising actors under Joan Littlewood and it swiftly became known for its politically progressive approach.

Corbett made slow but steady progress, at first very much based on the theatre but then adding television. He had to make sure that he was not to be confused with the well-known children's television entertainer Harry Corbett (with the puppet Sooty), so he added the middle H, which stood for nothing.

He made his West End début in 1956 and by the end of that decade he was being hailed as a new prospect in classical acting – the English Marlon Brando, it is said that at least one newspaper called him, presumably partly in respect of his Method training. He had also started a film career. At his death *The Times* paid tribute to his acting skills, drawing attention to his playing parts by Shakespeare and others. There can be no doubts that late in the 1950s his contribution to the classical theatre offered great promise.

But while appearing as Macbeth at the Bristol Old Vic in 1961, and having no idea of the very different future that lay before him, he accepted a part in a BBC comedy television play *The Offer*. It centred on two London rag-and-bone men, the other being played by Wilfred Brambell. The script was by the incomparable Galton and Simpson, fresh from years of *Hancock's Half-hour*. They later pointed to the fact that Corbett and Brambell were trained actors – not comics, who had previously led every comedy series – as crucial to the show's success. On Corbett's death, Simpson said, "He was the most inventive actor I have ever known – always looking at a line, word or an inflection to bring out a better meaning in it".

Seeing that they were on to a good thing, after *The Offer* the BBC commissioned the *Steptoe and Son* series that ran from 1962 to 1974 and has been frequently repeated. Comedy series usually take a little time to catch on but this was an immediate hit.

Much has been made of the real-life relationship of the two Steptoes. It has often been claimed that they hated each other, but this has been authoritatively denied by Corbett's daughter and by others. Certainly Brambell could be difficult, mainly because he drank to excess and this must have led to problems at the studio, but the two did get on well.

Corbett was a devoted supporter of the Labour Party, which may have been a factor in his being appointed OBE in 1976. This was an odd occasion in that those responsible mistakenly sent the invitation to the Sooty man; the only way out was for both of them to be appointed OBE.

During his *Steptoe and Son* period Corbett continued acting elsewhere, but he became stuck in light comedy roles. Rarely in the best of health, he had a heart attack in 1979 and another, fatally, in 1982. He is buried in Penhurst churchyard.

Corbett's local relationship began in 1972, when he bought the cottage at Penhurst to which the family – he, his wife Maureen and two children – moved five years later. He died at St Helen's Hospital at Hastings (the old workhouse) for which he had raised funds since they had successfully treated his first heart attack. A memorial service was held for him at St Paul's Church, Covent Garden.

His daughter Susannah is herself a well-known actor and the author of an immensely readable biography of her father. He had made 31 films, few of which are now shown.

5
Religion

Religious allegiance was so important up to and perhaps beyond the twentieth century one might have thought that there were memorable ministers of religion in every parish. Some appear in Chapter 1 but only five more men and one woman furnish this account.

He twice nearly became archbishop of Canterbury

Odo of Canterbury
(?–1200)

Odo, Abbot of Battle, might well have had the honour of primacy. His career demonstrates the education, drive and common sense of the best monks of his day.

After Thomas à Becket was murdered in December 1170, Henry II filled no vacant bishoprics or abbacies. Only in 1174 was Richard of Dover elected archbishop. Together with the King he filled bishopric vacancies; they then moved on to the abbacies.

Battle's Abbot Walter de Luci had died in 1171. The Archbishop wrote to every vacant abbey ordering their priors and some monks to Woodstock to elect new abbots. Battle was asked to bring the charters of privileges and exemptions granted by William I, and this inevitably led to concern about the potential implications. The Abbey selected two of those going to Woodstock as proposed 'home grown' abbots – two being nominated in case one was unacceptable.

Battle's Prior and four monks arrived at Woodstock and were called first. They met the Bishop of London and others for an exploratory meeting. The problem was that the King wouldn't accept either of Battle's nominees and had asked the monks to name another from a list of many possible candidates. The monks were in a dilemma. They didn't know anyone on the list and had been instructed by their chapter to elect one of their two nominees. By all accounts things got a little heated and the King came in angrily, asking why they were holding things up.

Prior Odo of Canterbury was there on another matter – the charters of Canterbury Abbey had been lost in a fire and he wished to model new charters on Battle's, which was why Battle had been asked to bring them.

Odo had become a monk at Christ Church, Canterbury and then a sub-prior in 1163. In that year he was sent by Archbishop Becket to the Pope as his representative to attend an appeal against the Archbishop of York who was continuing to act in the province of Canterbury. In 1167 he became prior.

In 1172 the Christ Church monks put Odo forward for the archbishopric. The King procrastinated. Odo and others followed Henry II to Normandy and urged that a monk should be chosen as archbishop. After long negotiations Richard, Prior of Dover and formerly a monk of Canterbury, was chosen and Odo wrote to the Pope on his behalf.

So in 1174 the Battle monks, knowing Odo's reputation, said that they would accept him as their abbot. The Bishop of London told the King and Archbishop and the monks made a long speech choosing Odo. But Odo refused: should he be forced, he would appeal to the Pope. He was argued with for a long time to make him change his mind and in the end he agreed. He wished to consult his brothers at Canterbury and they approved the appointment, saying that they would still wish to receive his counsel and aid.

Odo arrived at Battle in 1175. The monks and the people received him with apparent rapture. But he needed to be consecrated, and the Bishop of Chichester was soon on the scene, sending his dean to Battle to discuss the matter. The well-briefed Odo pointed to his Abbey's exclusion from the diocese. He sent the dean away and went to see the King and Archbishop. It was suggested that another bishop should bless Odo in the presence of the King, but Archbishop Richard obtained royal permission to bless the abbot-elect. He did this at his manor of Malling, by Lewes, which as another Peculiar lay outside of the jurisdiction of Chichester.

Odo was charming, eloquent and fluent in Latin, French and English. He was also a very able administrator. He had the ear of the King, who took his advice when appointing an abbot of St. Augustine's, Canterbury. Odo also mediated after the new Prior of Canterbury had upset the King; in due course that Prior was made Abbot of Peterborough. He showed the King one of the Abbey's charters of William I that had deteriorated with age and the King agreed that it needed renewing, but wouldn't agree to have it done except by judgement of his court. He took advice from Richard de Luci, who assured him that there would be no problem with this and in due course the court agreed.

It was normal for such charters, on being copied, to insert something to refer back to the earlier copy but in this instance, to avoid future challenge, the King wished the wording to be: *Since I have inspected the charter of William my ancestor, in which were contained the aforesaid liberties and exemptions and free customs given the church by him....* The King explained that if the normal phrase were used the later charter would confer little without the presence of the earlier, but now this charter alone would be enough even if all the earlier charters of Battle were lost. The Abbot received three copies of this new charter, each with the King's seal attached, to ensure that at least one copy was always at the Abbey.

Odo also wished to retrieve the manor of Wye from the de Luci family; it had historically belonged to Battle Abbey. He had great problems in finding an advocate, for many feared the de Lucis' powers. Even old friends refused to help. When at last an advocate was found, the case came before a legatine (a legate of the Pope) not a royal court. It ended in compromise with Richard de Luci's son left as vicar of Wye.

In Abbot Odo's time a new house or hospital was built for pilgrims and other travellers, just outside the Abbey gate. It stood behind a courtyard and some dwellings, with a gateway on to Abbey Green. Its fifteenth-century replacement is known as the Pilgrims' Rest.

In 1184 he was again put forward for the primacy of Canterbury but the King preferred a bishop with a Cistercian background. After this, there was a difficult struggle between the new archbishop and the almost self-governing monks of Canterbury, and Odo played a prominent part, acting on the Pope's behalf against the primate.

When Odo died he was buried in the lower part of the church at Battle Abbey, 'under a slab of black Lydian marble'. He was later venerated at Battle as a saint, and the Relic List at Canterbury Cathedral mentions 'a tooth of the Venerable Odo, Abbot of Battle'.

Odo was a lover of books and a great theologian. There is

Odo's tomb?
Photo: © K Foord.

uncertainty as to his writings, owing to confusion with others named Odo, but a list of thirteen works, chiefly writings on the Old Testament and on sermons, can be confidently ascribed to him. Two of his books remained in the library of Battle Abbey over 300 years later, at the dissolution in 1538.

Henry had found time to confirm Battle Abbey's charter, but not the sole right of the abbot to dispense justice within the defined area of the Abbey's authority: it was now increasingly to be shared with the itinerant justices.

The permitted Catholic leader

Magdalen, Viscountess Montagu
(1538–1608)

In late Elizabethan and early Stuart England it was often very dangerous to be a Roman Catholic even if not a priest. You could be aiding and abetting high treason and suffer an awful death. But one person carried on a peaceful if careful life, becoming a centre of Catholic life in the South East.

This was Magdalen Dacre, wife of the second Sir Anthony Browne of Battle Abbey who was made Viscount Montagu by Mary Tudor. Magdalen had been a maid of honour when Mary married the King of Spain and both Montagus were dedicated Catholics and remained so for the rest of their lives, even if that did not stop her husband from loyal service to Queen Elizabeth.

After his death in 1592 Magdalen lived mainly at Battle, one of three houses available to her. During Elizabeth's last decade she was pursued only once, when Robert Gray, a priest on her payroll, was being hunted.

Richard Smith was one of her confessors, active in Catholic affairs in Britain and abroad. He began his association with the Montagus from around 1603. This may explain why her harassment from the authorities was serious only during James I's reign. He became the second Vicar Apostolic of England in 1625.

Through the early years of the seventeenth century no fewer than three priests were resident in Battle; Thomas More (great-grandson of Sir Thomas), Thomas Smith and Richard Smith. Also near Battle were other recusant families such as the Pelhams of Catsfield and the Ashburnhams.

Lady Montagu was fairly open about her Catholic practices at Battle; so much so that Battle Abbey became known locally as 'Little

**Magdalen, Viscountess Montagu, manner of Antonis Mor
(1517–77),** from the Burghley Collection. © Burghley House
Preservation Trust Limited.

Rome', with a chantry, Masses and a number of communicants. The
novices' chamber may have been used for celebration of the Mass.
This chapel was described as sumptuous, complete with an elevated
altar and a choir.

One researcher quotes sources to describe the adverse impact on
conformist worship which Lady Montagu was perceived to be having
in the Battle area. The Dean of Battle, Dr John Wythines (Dean
1572–1615), was thought to be backward in the number of religious
ceremonies, particularly communions, being carried out in the Battle
locality, although it may be that he often left a curate in charge as
his wife and children lived elsewhere, possibly in Kent or Berkshire.
He had studied at Oxford and remained at the university in various
positions until he took up the post at Battle. His brass in St Mary's
church records his date of death at the age of 84. He appears to have
remained somewhat sympathetic to Catholicism.

A report entitled *An Account of the Dangerous Combinations of
Recusants in and about Battle in Sussex 1596* states (spelling of original
text preserved):

Informacons of certaine abuses in Sussex. Popery since the L.Montagu's coming to dwel at Battle, religion in that countrey, and especially in that towne, is greatly decayed, as may appear by these few poyntes. D. Witheris, Deane of Battle is suspected to be very backward in religion. For this two yeares and more he neither ministreth the communion nor receaueth it; but commonly, if there be a communion, he getteth some other to doe it, and either getteth himself out of the towne or keepeth his house. His wife cometh scarse twis a year to church and receauth not the communion, he hath a sonne and a daughter at man's estate, which neuver receauth the communion...... The jurisdiction of the place is in the deane, wholly exempt from the byshop's visitation, and is altogether neglected by him; soe that they doe what they list. There are many in the towne that never receauth the communion, and come very seldome at churche.

The notorious Catholic hunter, Richard Topcliffe, claimed to have found a holy well in Battle Park where women went as if on pilgrimage. (Evidence for this remains unclear.) There was a printing press, but it might have been at any of Lady Montagu's houses. Richard Smith said that she had three priests and she redeemed two others out of prison. According to his account it seems that she attended conformist services for a while, but "did abhor it … when she knew it to be unlawful..." He doesn't say she stopped going. It would have been a useful ploy.

The same document reports that the Dean kept the company of Lady Montagu and two men named Gray and Terry who had served time in prison for their beliefs, put there by Sir Francis Walsingham, Elizabeth's spymaster. Gray was a Catholic priest and Terry a schoolmaster at Battle.

It is likely that Gray taught at the Abbey, perhaps teaching Thomas Pilcher, the future martyr. It is also likely that Gregory Martin, the translator of the Bible, had some education at the Abbey. The most precise account of the authorities' attempts to deal with Lady Montagu herself is also at the end of the sixteenth century, from Richard Smith. As her priest he would, of course, be hoping that her persecutors would come to a bad end, but the accounts may be accurate.

Apprehension of individuals, inspections of properties and fines were among the approaches used against those suspected to be practising Masses or who had been insufficiently attending conformist services. On the other hand there were limits to central resources and how far the authorities could look into everything. Lady Montagu had good connections and it seems to have been possible to move individuals quite easily between her own properties and those of sympathetic families.

Sir Thomas May of Burwash tried to round up her servants to show they were priests in disguise but eventually he was imprisoned for debt. Another accuser, Nicholas Cobbe, also wound up being arrested on other charges. The third persecutor, Benet, cursed Lady Montagu on a market day in Battle but three days later he "fell into a pit at the town's end towards London". Richard Smith records with satisfaction that he was assumed to have committed suicide so was "buried like a dog at the roadside". We can only speculate as to the extent to which Lady Montagu may have played a part in these outcomes.

The role of Edward/Edmund Pelham is questionable. He appears to have acted as a protector of Lady Montagu and other Catholics in Sussex but was himself a recusancy commissioner in 1602. Lady Montagu had some credit at Court, even in the reign of James I: in 1607 the Privy Council decreed, in respect of her non-attendance at services, that there should be no sentence against her, "on the grounds of her status, age and former fidelity to Queen Elizabeth".

Smith relates a miracle – presumable at Battle – during Lady Montagu's time, when an altar stone fell on a woman but did not hurt her. (For those inclined to believe these things, it may be that this was just a warning from the Protestant God.) The extent of Lady Montagu's protection of her entourage is shown by the events after her death, when in 1610 Sir Barnard Whetstone headed a vigorous recusancy commission against her tenants and retainers.

The Catholic population of Battle shrank in the new century, perhaps partly because the Montagus preferred to live and worship at Cowdray House rather than at Battle. Once Viscountess Montagu died there would have been no active focus.

The Roman Catholic Bible translator

Gregory Martin
(c 1542–82)

Gregory Martin, artist unknown,

Martin was a scholar, translator and author in a time of great danger. He remained a Roman Catholic to the end of his short life, being instrumental in the founding of the English College at Rome. He had been born at Maxfield near Three Oaks, itself a tiny place in the parish of Guestling a little east of Hastings. Maxfield was the property of Battle Abbey.

It would seem that he received an excellent Catholic education, which may have been from the recusants centred on the Abbey under the Browne family. In a later letter to his sisters Gregory said only, *It pleased my parents to bring me up in learning.* He went to St John's

College, Oxford, founded in 1555 to provide a source of educated Roman Catholic priests to support the counter-reformation under Queen Mary. Martin was to spend 13 years at Oxford but left when things got too difficult for Catholics under Elizabeth I. He then tutored the children of the (Catholic) Duke of Norfolk at Arundel. Things now got worse, particularly after the Pope excommunicated the Queen in 1570. Martin left to join Dr William Allen's English College at Douai (then in the Spanish Netherlands), to train for the Catholic priesthood. He was ordained in 1573.

Originally the Douai college was intended for Catholics from England as a place where they could continue their studies in a way no longer possible at home. Allen recognised its potential for training priests ready for the return to England when 'the new religion' had run its course. Many, however, proved impatient to wait for that and Douai found itself dedicated largely to training missionary priests: 158 of its graduates were to meet a martyr's death.

Martin was not destined to be a missionary priest, with the hazards that that entailed. He was clearly a learned scholar and a Doctor of Divinity, not a man of action. Two years after ordination he went to Rome with Allen to found the English College there. He stayed for two years organising a course of studies but may have had some difficulties with entrenched personalities. Allen recalled him to his first college, now at Reims because of political troubles.

Allen announced in September 1578 that a Catholic version of the Bible in English was to be produced as part of the fightback against radical Protestantism, to help in the re-conversion of England.

Gregory Martin was the man chosen to do the new translation, using as a basis the Latin Vulgate Bible, the Bible approved by the Council of Trent, rather than the original Hebrew and Greek texts, which Gregory would still refer to. The difficulty with this was that if it proved difficult or even impossible to find a suitable English word, an anglicised Latin word would still be used. This made it cumbersome in places, but importantly to the translators it was accurate.

Interestingly, Allen's foreword to this Bible would show that the translators didn't really approve of making a version available in ordinary spoken languages, *as it was not always wise for just anyone to read the Bible, which they felt needed to be carefully explained by Church officials.* So this was a 'political' Bible and in parts it would address the critical need to answer Protestant interpretations because Protestants had published so many *erroneous* Bibles.

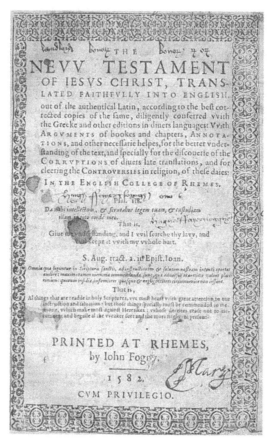

Title page from the 1582 Douai-Rheims New Testament

He undertook the vast bulk of the translation, working through the Old to the New Testaments at two chapters a day, with 1300 chapters to go – at that rate it would be just under two years' work. He was assisted by other priests, and by Allen himself in revisions and in preparing suitable notes to the passages of the Bible most used by Protestants to attack Catholics. Finally it was ready in July 1580. Early in 1582 the Reims New Testament was published with a foreword by Allen, but apparently Martin's drafting of this shows through.

At the same time he produced a contentious book of over 300 pages – *Discovery of the Manifold Corruptions of the Holy Scripture by the Heretikes of our Daies*. Doubtless, as intended, it provoked many and continuing Protestant replies.

His writings had taken their toll and he developed pulmonary tuberculosis. Allen sent him to Paris and Rouen to try a cure but it was too late. He returned to Reims to die in September 1582.

Allen went on to higher things, being created Cardinal in 1587. The college went back to Douai in 1593 but was dissolved during the French Revolution. The Douai–Reims Old Testament was not to be published until nearly 25 years after completion, in two volumes in 1609 and 1610.

The Elizabethan martyr

❦

Thomas Pilcher
(c 1556–1587)

Pilcher was a Catholic martyr hanged, drawn and quartered in the reign of Elizabeth I. It was a horrible death.

He came of an old-established Battle family (it long survived him) and it was a family not without some wealth. But his misfortune was to become a Catholic priest at a point when, the Queen having been excommunicated by the Pope, it was clear that the Catholic powers of the rest of Europe wanted her out, executed if she did not recant and probably even if she did.

The Brownes of Battle Abbey may have been instrumental in Pilcher's brief life, at least in his early education. He went to Balliol College, Oxford, regarded as a 'strong centre of papistry', and had a good career there. After graduation he became a Fellow of the college and also its bursar. But Richard Topcliffe got going after 1578, looking for Catholics everywhere and leading many to a dreadful death.

The Queen's spies must have been aware of the beliefs held by men at Balliol and would have been watching them. Perhaps they were not surprised when in 1580 Pilcher left to go to the English College at Reims to become a Catholic priest. His departure (and perhaps his arrival) was noticed by government agents. They were on the lookout for Catholic priests, for now their practice was regarded as high treason.

This did not deter Pilcher. He was ordained sub-deacon in 1582, deacon later that year and priest in 1583. He promptly left to work in the West Country. It must have been a lonely life, moving very frequently and in danger of identification by Protestants. In fact that is what must have happened, for he was arrested and imprisoned.

But in 1585, as an act of leniency, he was among 72 Catholic priests released and sent into permanent exile. If he returned there would be no defence against the charge of high treason.

Of course, this made no difference to his resolve to promote the re-conversion of his native country, and after a short time at Reims he left for England again in January 1586, being smuggled back in under the surname Pilchard. Although again based in the West Country, it was in London that he was recognised by a fellow Oxford man, arrested and sent for trial at Dorchester. He must have known that death at the hands of an executioner was inevitable. On 21 March he was found guilty of high treason and sentenced to die on the same day.

An anonymous execution, probably of a later date. On the left the victim's leg is being burned.

Executions for felonies were particularly nasty events. He was roughly dragged on a hurdle from the prison to the site of execution; a sympathetic Protestant minister said to him *oportet te gloriari in Christo* (You must glory in Christ). By the time he arrived he was in a poor state and fainting, but still able to speak on the scaffold, again showing great piety. The usual hangman wasn't available and a cook had to perform the sentence. While Pilcher was hanging, the rope either broke or was cut too soon but he was still conscious enough to stand. At this point the cook had to be goaded to carry on but then, due to his inexperience or possibly cruelty, he prolonged the process of disembowelling, at which the crowd cried out to him to finish the agony rapidly. Thomas was heard to utter the words *miserere mei* and one account suggests that he even cast out his own intestines. His body was finally quartered.

Thomas Pilcher's terrible death is not easily forgotten. He was declared a martyr by Pope Leo XIII on 4 December 1886.

The very busy Non-conformist

❧❦

William Vidler
(1758–1816)

Vidler was a noted preacher, first of the Baptist denomination and then of what became Unitarianism. Nothing could keep him down. He was a major Non-conformist of the age then opening. From an early age he became a remarkably influential figure in Non-conformist circles. Born at Battle, he would be intimately involved in the growth and definition of not just one denomination but two.

Vidler's family were Anglican, and the Dean of Battle identified the young man as intelligent and eager to learn, and arranged for him to stay with his brother on the Isle of Wight. He was to learn 'theology and the art to declaim it', Biblical languages and 'theological arts'. No doubt he did learn things but his Anglicanism came to an end after he came under the influence of an Independent Calvinist from Heathfield, George Gilbert (the 'Apostle of Sussex').

Gilbert came to Battle to hold services in January 1776. He preached to about 40 people and "the Word seemed to be well received." Gilbert had charisma. Once regarded as a wild, reckless and immoral soldier, he had converted to Methodism and became an overseer on the Heathfield Park estate of his former commanding officer. He went around Sussex villages conducting religious meetings.

He came to Battle again in March 1776, after which the landlord concerned forbade preaching (was it was too loud?) and a 'conversation' took place instead. "Several persons seemed to be in earnest about their salvation, the appearance of which set the whole town in confusion." Following later visits in 1776, when Gilbert preached under the Watch Oak at the north end of the town, a small group formed an Independent Calvinist Church. They gathered

A young William Vidler
from uuddb.org

regularly for worship, initially worshipping in a room of a house on 'The Mount'. The Dean tried to keep Vidler in the conformist fold but he joined this church. In 1777 he started lay-preaching.

The historian of the Battle Baptists records:

> The newly-formed band of disciples gathered by Gilbert recalled William ... to be their leader at £17 per year, and amongst those who attended his first meeting as pastor were representatives from Sedlescombe of 'the pious Lady Huntingdon' Connexion, some Quakers from Lewes, George Gilbert of Heathfield, and Thomas Purdy, for fifty or more years Baptist Pastor at Rye.

The number of members rose rapidly from 15 to 150 and, in 1780, a majority of this church re-organised as a Baptist Calvinist Church and made Vidler minister. By 1782 they had bought a house described as 'the old Presbyterian building'. They pulled it down in 1789 and bought part of an adjacent orchard for £60. This left them in debt for the land, but most of this was found from members and friends. Then they built a new chapel that opened in 1789/90 but left them with a debt of £700. According to nineteenth-century maps, this chapel stood on the same side as today's Zion Chapel but a little further up Mount Street, set back some distance from the road, at the corner of what is now the Mountjoy road.

The Battle Unitarian Chapel, formerly Baptist, from a newspaper photograph

Vidler was a powerful preacher, often travelling to villages near Battle and preaching in the open air. He met insults, particularly when he carried out baptismal services in local streams and ponds. Some of this hostility was encouraged by people from the 'better classes'. But he is said to have shown a constant good humour and wit of reply to enable attacks to be turned, sometimes to good account.

He was a voracious reader and soon came across Elhanan Winchester's *Dialogues on the Universal Restoration*, published in 1788. Winchester was an American who had adopted the doctrine of Universal Restoration, revived in 1750. He had come to England to spread his theories and by 1787 had drawn together a large and influential congregation in the City. Vidler met Winchester's followers in Lincolnshire and returned to Battle a strong believer in the universal restoration of all humankind.

In 1791 he toured Baptist churches to collect funds for the Battle chapel. He had little success in whittling down the £700 still owed but the travels allowed him to time to think, perhaps a bit too much.

He took the opportunity to test *"serious thoughts of the Godhead of Christ and the eternity of hell torments"*. His ideas were radical and by the end of 1792 he professed Universalism. *"It is long since I wrote anything of the state of my soul"*, he wrote in his diary on 22 August 1792. *"I have lately been much stirred up again by reading Mr. Winchester on the final restoration of all things, which doctrine … I am constrained to say I believe."*

This led to turmoil in the Baptist Calvinist Church at Battle. A huge debate took place at the end of 1792, followed by schism. A large majority loyally remained with Vidler as Universalists and some later became Unitarians, but 15 people left the Church and continued as Particular Baptists. So the Universalist majority kept the chapel. They also kept the debt, which would not be paid off for a very long time. After 1793 the chapel was renamed, and later had the legend over the entrance 'UNITARIAN CHAPEL – A. D. 1789'.

In the summer of 1793 the local Baptist association expelled and excommunicated Vidler and his Universalist congregation. The Minute Book of the Baptist Church at Rye states:

> July 1st 1793. At a quarterly Church meeting agreed to disown the Church at Battle as a sister church on account of Mr. William Vidler and many of his people imbibing the erroneous doctrine of Universal Restoration.

So now there were two Non-conformist churches in Battle: Vidler's Universal Baptists who would later become Unitarians, and the rump of Particular Baptists. The latter might claim that they were the continuity of the Particular Baptist church formed in 1780, but they had lost their chapel. The Universalists had it, together with the debt, with William Vidler as their pastor. They were the first regular church in England to declare for Universalism.

But Vidler was about to move elsewhere.

Winchester had preached at Parliament Court in the City from 1792 and asked Vidler to assist him there from February 1794; later that year he returned to America and Vidler succeeded him. He still gave half his time to Battle until November 1796, but after then he turned his attention beyond Sussex.

With a former minister of the General Baptist Church at Wisbech he played a significant role in establishing institutions that Unitarians still use today. Vidler had become a famed preacher and crowds came to hear him. In 1797 he published a magazine at first called *The Universalist Miscellany* and would edit it until 1815. In 1798 he was involved in revising a New Testament translated from the original Greek, which has been described as 'a useful curiosity' in that it presented dialogues dramatically. In 1804 he founded the Unitarian Evangelical Society and from 1806 he was travelling widely for the Unitarian Fund. He seems to have had great intellectual energy. Even in later life he was learning Latin for the first time and reading the many works of Joseph Priestley (the 18th century theologian and scientist who assisted in founding Unitarianism in England).

Vidler became very fat and always booked two seats when journeying by coach. Returning to London from Wisbech in 1808 to see his dying wife, his coach fell down a steep bank. He was injured and never fully recovered and thereafter he preached sitting down. He went to live in West Ham and died there. He said of himself:

Whatever changes I have gone through, whatever errors I may have held, I have this satisfaction, that I have ever held fast my integrity.

Unitarians had considerable influence in the nineteenth century due to their strongly-held progressive views. But their numbers fell and Battle Unitarian Chapel closed in 1898. The site was much later bought for extension by the next-door Baptist Chapel, which remains devoted to its original purpose. One might say that Vidler's side of the argument lost the contest.

The Catholic Carlist Earl

❦

Bertram, fifth Earl of Ashburnham
(1840–1913)

Tucked away off the road between Battle and Lewes sit the remnants of Ashburnham Place. The house standing there before its partial demolition is said to have had 365 rooms; it had a most elegant and attractive central hall with stairs and galleries designed by Charles Dance. Dating originally from 1665 (presumably on the site of or close to an earlier house) it was substantially rebuilt in Palladian style in the mid-eighteenth century; perhaps unfortunately it was faced with brick a hundred years later. Robert Adam designed the entrance lodges. The orangery and the estate were by Lancelot 'Capability' Brown.

Most of the house went after the last Ashburnham, Lady Catherine, died in 1953, an unmarried daughter who had been ineligible to inherit the earldom. The condition of the house – badly damaged by a bomb-laden plane in the Second World War – and very large death duties meant that there was no money for repairs even if a use could be found for such a palace. By 1959 most of it had been demolished. It is now home to the Ashburnham Christian Trust, founded by a cousin of the last owner, It is a non-denominational charity offering, among other things, the possibility of a degree in theology.

The Ashburnham family had been there for longer than any other land-owning family for a long way around. They had much land in the area. Usually staying out of national matters they only occasionally ran into trouble. The first was a financial problem that led to the estate being sequestrated from 1598 (they failed to pay the taxes levied on Catholic recusants) but then came the civil war.

John Ashburnham was close to Charles I. He was not only a devoted Royalist but Groom of the Bedchamber. He stayed with the King and at one point helped him to escape, but he was recaptured. He attended the King's execution, and some of Charles's possessions came to the family, including the sheet on which the King's body was laid, his drawers and the bloodstained shirt he was wearing when the axe fell. (It is now in the Museum of London.)

Ashburnham's loyalty never waned. During the Commonwealth he lost the remainder of his lands and spent five years in close confinement, with three banishments to Guernsey. Charles II restored all the lands after the Restoration. The family was now Anglican.

They were not just traditional landowners: they were also heavily involved in the iron-smelting industry. They began it at Ashburnham in 1549 and kept the last furnace in Sussex, closing it as late as 1813. Their first peerage was in 1689, after their support for William and Mary against James II. The earldom followed in 1730. The family continued to increase their lands; the controversial fifth earl had some 24,000 acres when he died.

He succeeded to the title and estates in 1878 and became well-known, perhaps notorious, for his political and religious activities. It isn't known why in 1872 he threw over recent family tradition and converted to Roman Catholicism. Like so many converts to a new faith, he was very eager indeed in its promotion and defence. It took him in some controversial directions, including an involvement in Spanish politics on the side of Carlism.

A Carlist flag, c. 1875

Carlism was a major issue in nineteenth-century Spain, which like Portugal, had allowed a daughter to succeed to the throne. The would-be absolutist King Carlos had expected to succeed and took exception to his exclusion in favour of a woman. He gathered support from a variety of sources, including much of the Catholic Church and from many landowners, all of whom were threatened by a rising liberal tide. He also attracted significant minorities such as the Basques, whose provincial liberties were always in danger of abrogation. There were four Carlist wars: 1833–40, 1847–49 and 1872–76, with another attempt at the turn of the century. The reactionaries were defeated in all of them, but continued as something of a force in the land.

Bertram Ashburnham, the fifth Earl

The earl was the strongest British Carlist. He worked tirelessly for the cause. The last Carlist opportunity followed the catastrophe of the Spanish–American war of 1898–99, in which Spain lost Cuba and its Pacific properties.

Ashburnham helped it by allowing military training on his Welsh estates and by supplying a yacht to carry arms and men to a trusted Spanish port. The French intercepted it at Arcachon and found it to be carrying 3664 rifles. The captain was convicted of failing to make a proper declaration of the cargo, and although the ship and men were allowed to go back to Southampton the rifles were detained. Newspapers made no mention of Ashburnham, but it has been established that it was he who provided both yacht and weaponry and allowed his lands to be used.

The Earl was not only a Carlist. His fervent Catholicism led him to found a neo-Jacobite group and to give vigorous support to Irish home rule. He worshipped at home: the Catholic chapel at Ashburnham Place continued in use up to the Earl's death in 1913, again after the death of the sixth and last earl in 1924, and up to 1953 when a requiem Mass was said there for his daughter.

The Earl's faith produced the Battle Roman Catholic church in Mount Street. In about 1882 he bought the house known as The Hollies, ironically once the home of the prominent Baptist Richard Sinnock, and founded a Catholic school there; the church was built in its garden and opened in February 1888. For his efforts, the Earl became the Senior Knight of the Holy Sepulchre in Great Britain and was awarded the Grand Cross of Sovereign Order of St John of Jerusalem and the Pontifical Order of Pius, all papal honours.

Whatever his virtues or faults, it was unfortunate that he disposed of a large proportion of the artistic and literary collections amassed by the family over the years. He offered them to the British Museum but his price of £90,000 was too high, though there is a report that trustees would make up the difference between that and the £70,000 the government was prepared to pay. So most went privately. The collection included a famous Rembrandt that went for well below its real market value (and in 1911 it was sold on for £20,000), a library containing unique works of great value and a collection of mediaeval miniatures that had been described as the 'unquestionably the finest collection of its kind in the world'. Ashburnham House in Dover Street, off Piccadilly, also went.

The Earl had two children but neither was destined to succeed him in the peerage. His son died as an infant; the other, being female, could not do so. So a brother took the earldom, being the last Earl of Ashburnham. His daughter, Lady Catherine, was the last Ashburnham to live in the great house. It had been left to her by her father on condition that she did not continue her progress towards becoming a nun.

6

❧

English royalty

Very few English kings had significant connections with Battle after the Conqueror left, but two did.

Father and son
who started civil wars

❦

John (1199–2016)
and Henry III (1216–72)

England has had perhaps many difficult monarchs but John and his son Henry each managed to spark a civil war. The father may have murdered his elder brother to obtain the throne; his son was responsible for a mass murder of innocent men. Both had connections with the Battle area.

John can be remembered for renewing Battle Abbey's charter favourably, guaranteeing its freedom from the Chichester diocese and allowing it to elect its own abbot. There were terms, however: in return it cost the abbey £1,000. It's hard to be sure how much that means in today's money but clearly at the very least approaching a million and perhaps anything up to about £400 million – a good indication not only of his need for money to rebuild his armed forces but also of the Abbey's wealth.

Unusually for a king, he visited Battle at least three times. Travelling around the country was one way of trying to keep his many barons in order, something that was to prove unsuccessful. He may also have visited Hastings in 1201 to issue the *Ordinance of the Sea*, later transcribed into the *Black Book of the Admiralty* containing naval regulations, the *Laws of Oléron* (basic early seafaring rules), another three ordinances issued by John, and other ordinances of Henry I, Richard I and Edward I. It demanded that if a king's ship were to meet another ship the latter should strike its flag or lower its topsail, or be regarded as an enemy. This probably derived from his having land on each side of the English Channel: so anyone was crossing 'his' waters, but he was soon to lose his lands in northern France.

It is likely that John gained over £100,000 in the money of the day at the expense of the church, a colossal sum. Many abbeys had bribed him to allow them to perform services in defiance of a papal interdict, and he also took the profits from their lands and property over the whole period, only ever repaying about half the money he received. Battle Abbey did not pay him and went through a very difficult period.

Kings were always prone to go to war. But war is an expensive business, and popular only if it succeeds in some way. John was unlucky, incompetent or both. By 1206 he had lost large parts of France and wanted to win them back. Taxes were increased, and he used his feudal rights in 'innovative' ways to extract even more money from the barons and elsewhere. It worked to some extent but didn't result in any reversal of the land losses.

In July 1214 the English army and its allies suffered total defeat at the hands of the French at the Battle of Bouvines. The expense had been useless. Enormous baronial discontent eventually led to John facing them at Runnymede and signing the Magna Carta in 1215. Of course John claimed that he had signed under duress and in the following year civil war broke out.

The barons were desperate and wanted John out. They invited

Tomb effigy of King John, Winchester Cathedral.
From Samuel R Gardner, *History of England*

his nephew by marriage to invade the country: Prince Louis, later King of France. He landed at Sandwich in May 2016 and reached London early in June, but perhaps prudently no-one could be found to crown him. The inevitable war came to an end with John's death in October.

By now his son and heir Henry had only just turned nine and the barons ran the country. For a time they could breathe more easily.

But when allowed to rule Henry showed himself possibly a bigger disaster than his father, and he was probably more murderous. He didn't mean to surrender so much of his power to a parliament but he was forced to do so by a battle in Sussex.

From his age of majority he began to attract opposition. He gave what the barons saw as excessive favours to foreigners rather than to themselves, and of course he wanted money for wars. Abbot Ralph of Battle from 1235, who was already facing heavy demands from the Pope, was among the ecclesiastical spokesman for the opposition:

A contemporary writer assures us that '*the large sum of 200 marks has been claimed and recovered from this convent*' and '*... notwithstanding the severe extractions they had suffered at the hands of his minions, who had, under various pretexts, levied unheard of contributions on the ecclesiastics of the kingdom*'.

Discontent rose to a head, again over taxes to support wars. Henry had levied extortionate taxes for war with Wales and more failed campaigns in France (and extensive ecclesiastical building, including the rebuilding of Westminster Abbey). The last straw was his agreement to cover the debts of the Pope in a fruitless war with Sicily. The barons demanded sweeping reforms and Henry was in no position to resist. In 1258 he agreed to place them in virtual control of the realm through a council of 15 men, without whose consent Henry could do very little. The scene was being set for conflict, but also created a precedent which would curtail the authority of all future English monarchs. The barons initiated a three-year period of reform, with new processes affecting justice, finance and the role of foreigners.

But in 1259/60 Henry was in France, an absence that enabled him to evade the reformers' work, and many of his opponents lost heart. Support for them was evaporating. As his father had done with the

1215 Magna Carta, Henry obtained a papal bull proclaiming the reforms unconstitutional. He began to reassert his authority and, by late 1261, most reformers had acquiesced. The chief reformer Simon de Montfort, Earl of Leicester and Henry's brother-in-law, returned to his native France.

Enough discontented barons survived to encourage de Montfort to return. He gathered supporters and generally made himself a thorough nuisance. Arbitration failed and a full civil war broke out; Sussex was to be the turning point for Henry and indeed for England.

The barons' leaders were de Montfort and Gilbert de Clare, Earl of Gloucester. Each had some connection with the county, both holding manors in eastern Sussex. London too was held by the barons and strongly favoured their cause. Reinforced by a large contingent of Londoners, the two barons left London on 6 May 1264 and marched in the direction of Lewes.

Henry decided to focus his forces where they would have the support of the local lords. Sussex appeared a good choice. Lewes Castle was in the hands of the King's brother-in-law, Pevensey and Hastings were held by an uncle and the barons of Bramber and Arundel had both proved their loyalty in the defence of Rochester Castle. In early May his army moved southwards with the aim of securing the Cinque Ports and the coast.

En route they stopped overnight at Combwell Priory just north of Flimwell, where one of the King's cooks, 'Master Thomas', is reported to have been murdered. The reprisal was an act of terror, unusually severe even for its time. 315 archers were beheaded in the presence of the king, all of whom had been called deceitfully to him.

Moving on to Robertsbridge Abbey and still in an angry mood, Henry, his son Lord Edward and their company were entertained but obliged the monks to pay a heavy ransom of 500 marks (£333) to Edward to spare their lives.

On the next day, the abbot and brothers of Battle Abbey went out in procession (presumably in considerable trepidation) to meet the King and give him a loyal welcome. Henry was still angry and demanded 100 marks (£66.67) from the abbey. He said that some of its tenants had been in the Flimwell area at the time of Master Thomas's death – not that the Abbey was in a position to forbid them to go wherever they wished. His heir Edward demanded another 40 marks, and some damage was inflicted on the Abbey's goods. Compared to Combwell and Robertsbridge they got off lightly.

On 4 May the King went to Winchelsea to ensure the support of the Cinque Ports. This was not forthcoming so he took hostages, who gave a grudging promise to obtain ships for the King's use. His army was let loose on the wine cellars, with predictable results. After four days he returned to Battle, and received news that the barons were assembling near Lewes. So he moved westwards, reaching Lewes by way of Herstmonceux on 10/11 May. Henry lodged at the priory and the castle defences were bolstered with his troops.

The barons had encamped at Fletching, some eight miles away. Negotiations failed and so the Battle of Lewes took place. The barons won and Henry and the Lord Edward were taken prisoner.

Edward was sent to Dover castle. Simon de Montfort brought Henry back to Battle Abbey, 'no longer with power to extort money from his entertainers as he had done on his last visit less than a fortnight before', and thence to London, but not before Henry signed royal orders at Battle for a new governor of Windsor castle and for the release of many prisoners, including de Montfort's son, also called Simon. One commentator remarks:

> ... the monks must have relished the spectacle of speedy retribution, which now brought the wrong-doer humiliated and harmless to their door. Henry and his eldest son, Edward, along with his brother, Richard, earl of Cornwall, were placed under house arrest.

On 15 May some constitutional agreements were made or re-enacted. Henry and Edward were placed under house arrest.

De Montfort took control of the government 'in the name of the King' but realised the need to obtain wide support. He summoned barons from the whole country to an early pre-Parliament and in 1265 it invited burgesses from selected towns. Now the King had no choice, and agreed to update Magna Carta, but his son and heir Edward had escaped from confinement. Royalists continued to fight, and the ensuing war resulted in de Montfort's death at the battle of Evesham in 1265.

The Cinque Ports did not escape retribution for their support of the barons, although Rye and Hastings made 'grovelling apologies' in letters to the King. Winchelsea did not apologise. In late 1265/early 1266 Edward recruited ships from the east coast and the town was subjected to a combined attack from the sea and land. The leading citizens were 'put to the sword' but most people were spared. When Winchelsea again revolted in a smaller way in 1267, the result was the same.

The *Dictum of Kenilworth* of October 1266 was an accord with the rebels. It marked the end of the reform movement and the restoration of royal power, but many of the reforms passed by Simon de Montfort's parliaments were accepted by the King.

His authority was finally restored by the *Statute of Marlborough* (1267), in which he promised to uphold the latest version of Magna Carta and some of the earlier agreements. Magna Carta forms part of the Common Law today and is still in force where not abandoned or amended by Parliament (as a recent case showed). Sussex quieted after the excitements of the previous few years. The Parliament already established would remain with us to this day, with its various changes over the years.

7

⚜

Science, technology and exploration

Back in the old days there was little science education, and science itself was generally very primitive. By 1600 there had been considerable work on astronomy, however (though by no means as much as would dislodge astrology) and a little on medicine. There was virtually none on natural history, biology, chemistry or physics. What science existed was rarely subjected to the modern method of repeated testing in conditions that would allow reasonable conclusions to be reached. In England that had to wait for Francis Bacon's work of 1618.

The contribution of people of the Battle area to science and technology was very limited. But as time went on things got better. From the late seventeenth century scientific enquiry assumed its modern form.

As to exploration, accurate and public reporting of what people found – if they survived – began as late as the eighteenth century.

The Catsfield naturalist

❧☙

William Markwick, later Eversfield
(1739–1813)

ere was a man very much of the modern style: acute observation of the natural world.

Markwick was a wealthy landowner of Catsfield. His is not a famous name other than to specialists, either in his or our time, but endures because of his deep observations of flora and fauna and his consequent association with the late Gilbert White of Selborne.

Few observers of the natural world at that time were without substantial resources – they had to have the time for their pursuit and for the education to write about it – and Markwick was no exception. He came from a well-known Sussex family whose earliest records are connected with the Jevington area, near Eastbourne.

The family came to Catsfield late in the seventeenth century, and William was born there, son of James Markwick and Mary Eversfield; the Eversfields were a major landowning family of northern and eastern Sussex. Their family home was Catsfield Manor next to and behind the parish church.

William set out to be a barrister but didn't complete his Cambridge degree or pursue the law. There was no need for him to do so when he had sufficient means and wished to remain in the countryside. He had an estate of some 1600 acres stretching from Hastings to Eastbourne and as a country gentleman he was involved in local affairs as a magistrate and Deputy Lieutenant for the county.

He began his observations before he was 30. His natural history diary dates from or before 1768 when, just like Gilbert White at the same time, he noted down the times of the year at which birds and insects appeared and disappeared and plants and trees put out their leaves and flowers. He did not rush into print: his first known publication was dated 1791. He was conversant with Latin, of course, and translated some of Linnaeus's work into English. He was also a good artist, an essential quality for someone describing the natural world. His *Aves Sussexienses* of 1795 was the first study of Sussex birdlife.

Red Godwits: from a watercolour by William Markwick

Much of Markwick's land was on the Pevensey Levels and along the coast, and he was particularly interested in marshland and wading birds, fish and jellyfish as well as being a competent botanist and artist. He wrote articles for publication in the Transactions of the Linnaean Society: six papers between the years 1789 to 1801. He also submitted papers in 1797, 1800, 1806 and 1807, which remain in manuscript form. He also obviously sent specimens to the Society, evidenced by an amusing letter in their collections dated from Catsfield 28 January 1795, which read:

You may remember that in the year 1789 I sent you a specimen of the Scaup Duck [*Anas Marila*] together with the Tippet Grebe [*Podiceps Cristatus*], but your Servants thinking them Delicacies for the Table dressed them for your Dinner, before you could examine them as a Naturalist.

He became a Fellow of the Linnaean Society in 1792 and as well as papers he sent it further specimens of a male and female Scaup Duck.

On one occasion while copying extracts from the English translation (1786) of Count Buffon's *Histoire Naturelle des Oiseaux* (1770–86) in 1796 he noted Buffon's comments on the value of the beaks of birds such as the Crossbill, which he called 'a deformity', and of the Black Skimmer 'an awkward and defective instrument'. Markwick correctly pointed out that these were "admirably well formed" for their specific purposes and rebuked Buffon for "finding fault with the works of the Creator".

His data were published alongside the similar records collected by his older contemporary, the Rev. Gilbert White (1720–93). As far as we know Markwick and White never met or corresponded, in spite of the fact that they had so many interests in common, and the first edition of White's *The Natural History and Antiquities of Selborne* does not mention him. However, the 1802 second edition, edited by White's nephew, included and acknowledged his additions. Markwick's pioneering work in phenology, the study of when annual events happen in nature, formed part of the additions. Some 500 of his detailed observations are in this edition and it was praised as "a work of great exactness, and the result of as much, and as patient observation as perhaps was ever brought to the subject". It covered a comparison of the seasons, from 1768 to 1793. It declared that the additions were obtained through "the kindness of William Markwick, Esq., FLS, well known as an *accurate observer of nature*". A note in the second edition reads:

William Markwick … derived from his residence in the country opportunities of observing nature, which he embraced with a readiness worthy of a pupil of Gilbert White. His Naturalist's Calendar affords ample evidence of his perseverance in attending to and noting occurrences in both the organized kingdoms of the creation; and the remarks subjoined by him, in numerous instances, to our author's Observations on various Parts of Nature, shew him to have been a sensible as well as a diligent observer. He communicated to the Linnaean Society various essays on subjects of interest to the British zoologist, which were published in the earlier volumes of the Transactions of that body: the first of them, On the Migration of certain Birds, and on other Matters relating to the Feathered Tribes, included a Table of the annual appearance and disappearance of certain birds, which was continued to the end of 1794 in a subsequent communication, entitled Aves Sussexienses; or, a Catalogue of Birds found in the County of Sussex, with Remarks.

His last paper was *Observations on the Clover Weevil*, published in 1801.

In 1789, at the age of 50, Markwick had married Mary Date of Southampton, and they had four children. The connection with Catsfield was not to last, however. His uncle Sir Charles Eversfield of Denne Park, Horsham and The Grove, Hastings, died unmarried in October 1784 and his baronetcy expired. Sir Charles's sister Olive, also sister to Markwick's mother, survived him but it seems that the properties were held in an Eversfield trust. In 1803 Markwick received a legacy from Olive on condition that he changed his surname to hers, which he did. The legacy was complicated and legal matters associated with it occupied his time for some years.

He eventually achieved the inheritance of Denne Park, which still stands though much altered. When he died his son Charles continued to live at Catsfield, where he died in 1818, but his other son James preferred Denne.

Catsfield Manor was sold in 1826. Much of the land in west Hastings was also sold and allowed the development of St Leonards. Name evidence persists there with roads such as Eversfield Place and the appropriately named Markwick Gardens.

The Markwick manuscripts in the Linnaean Society archives have been catalogued and the contents listed. Perhaps they will now be edited in conjunction with the material at Hastings Museum, which holds 46 volumes containing his hand-written records and 'scrapbooks' from books and newspapers. One hopes that all these will be published, giving Markwick the recognition he deserves.

He invented the power loom

⚜️

Edmund Cartwright
(1743–1823)

Cartwright has a somewhat shaky connection with Battle.
Within the church of St Mary is the memorial to the inventor of the power loom, the Rev.Dr Edmund Cartwright, DD FRS. He obtained patents on the design of power looms in 1785 and 1787, but resistance to their introduction caused him to be bankrupted in 1793. His patents expired but he was eventually awarded £10,000 by Parliament which enabled him to retire to Hollenden in Kent at the age of seventy. He died in 1823 while in Hastings on a fashionable sea-bathing visit and was only fortuitously buried at Battle as the then Dean appears to have been a close friend.

Cartwright was one of those clergymen whose interests went far beyond the Church, like his contemporary Robert Young who almost deciphered the Rosetta stone and whose observations ultimately led to quantum theory.

He was the son of a knight. An Oxford graduate, he became rector of Goadby Marwood in Leicestershire, a few miles north of Melton Mowbray. Both his brothers were well-known – John (1740-1824), who was a strong proponent of parliamentary reform from as early as 1777, and whose proposals anticipated those of the Chartists sixty years later; and George (1740-1819), a soldier and an early explorer of Labrador.

Goadby Marwood is a very small village and would not have been much bigger then. Cartwright wrote poetry but his real interest was in technology. He must have had time on his hands, and he used it well. In the 1780s he experimented with applying power to looms used in weaving. Why he did so is unclear, but the experiments worked, and in 1789 he patented one that quickly appealed to manufacturers. It did so because it was fast and efficient and needed many fewer staff than any of the then existing looms (a factor that

EDMUND CARTWRIGHT, D.D. F.R.S.
MEMBER OF THE ROYAL SOCIETY
OF LITERATURE,
FORMERLY FELLOW OF
MAGDALEN COLLEGE OXFORD,
AFTERWARDS
RECTOR OF GOADBY MARWOOD
IN LEICESTERSHIRE,
AND PREBENDARY OF LINCOLN,
BORN APRIL 24ᵗʰ 1743,
DIED OCTOBER 30ᵗʰ 1823.

In a period of great intellectual advancement Doctor Cartwright both as a Poet and a Man of Science, possessed high claims to distinction ——— He published his first Poem "Armine and Elvira" in the year 1770. He was afterwards eminent for his mechanical discoveries which have proved of great national advantage, from their introduction into most of the principal manufactures. By these exertions of his very powerful genius he acquired the lasting friendship and respect of many of the most illustrious characters of this and other countries.

Nor should it be here omitted that, unbroken in mind by many severe disappointments, he retained through life an habitual equanimity: occupied to the last in a constant endeavour to improve and simplify the useful arts, and always studious to promote the benefit of mankind.

This Monument is erected to his memory by his affectionate and afflicted Widow

SUSANNAH CARTWRIGHT

In St Mary's Church, Battle. The plaque is surrounded by verses. Photo: Peter Greene.

was to cause unrest). It was taken up from 1790. For his work he was awarded his parliamentary grant – a very large sum for those days. Less popularly with manufacturers he invented machines for rope-making and wool-combing. He also seems to have invented a steam machine using alcohol rather than water. He was elected a Fellow of the Royal Society.

His son, also Edmund, followed him into Holy Orders and was rector of various Sussex parishes, which could explain Cartwright's death at Hastings – though all his son's parishes were well to the west (he wrote *A History of the Rape of Bramber*).

The then Dean of Battle, Thomas Birch, had no recorded connection with him, though there must have been one. Cartwright was a Fellow of an Oxford college and Birch, a Cambridge man, so they may have met when curates.

He invented the electric telegraph

❧❧

Sir Francis Ronalds
(1788–1873)

Ronalds's remains lie in Battle cemetery. He was a well-known nineteenth-century scientist and the brother-in-law of Samuel Carter, who built Telham Court (now Glengorse), and like him, a Unitarian.

Francis is best known for his work on the electric telegraph. It is probably now not well-known just how revolutionary the telegraph was. It allowed people to communicate almost instantly across any distance and in all weathers, in codes easily translatable into written languages. Before then the only such method was by semaphore signalling, a laborious, line-of-sight system relying on each signaller being able clearly to see the next one in line, provided there was daylight; this was the process by which urgent messages were sent between London and Portsmouth, for example, during the Napoleonic wars. It was, however, preferable to the earlier use of simple beacons, which would indicate only that there was some form of emergency. The heliograph, which made use of sunlight signals from mirrors, appeared only in the 1820s and relied on the sun actually showing itself.

But the telegraph was the marvel of the age. In 1845, for example, as recorded in Chapter 8, a fleeing murderer caught a train at Slough but had been noticed; when he arrived at Paddington the police were waiting for him, the telegraph having being used to warn them.

By the early nineteenth century electricity was beginning to be understood. The existence of positive and negative charges was known – the basis of all subsequent developments – and there were copper/zinc batteries on the galvanic principle. But its practical use was barely exploited. Faraday had not yet found electromagnetic induction and it took a long time for it to be used outside the laboratory; circuitry was not understood until rather later.

Ronalds had therefore to work with galvanic electricity. He created his telegraph in 1816, when he was 28. It was crude but it worked. He erected two frames in the large back garden behind his house in Chiswick, on which he built eight miles of wire, creating electricity by synchronously revolving discs. He then developed another version in which the wires were buried, having been encased in glass tubes. At each end of the line a clockwork mechanism turned synchronously revolving discs with letters on them. A frictional electricity machine kept the wire continuously charged, while at each end two pith balls hung from the wire on silk threads, and since they were similarly charged from the wire they stayed apart.

To send a message required someone to earth the wire at one end when a dial was set to a particular letter; the dial was linked to one at the other end and they always showed the same letter. At the receiving end the pith balls would fall together when earthed and the recipient noted the letter showing on his dial at that moment. It worked for over 150 metres of wire.

Convinced of the potential usefulness of his telegraph, he asked the Admiralty for support. It was the wrong moment. The Napoleonic wars had just ended, and it is likely that the Admiralty could see no way in which a wire-based model could communicate with ships though it might replace the semaphore system on land. There were some who thought that, with the war ended, telegraphs of any kind were now wholly unnecessary. (One is put in mind of those senior army officers who a century later associated tanks with the peculiar conditions of trench warfare and believed that the future, like the past, belonged to the horse.)

Actually there were good reasons for the Admiralty's rejection. A more reliable source of electricity was needed; the coding system was too slow; and glass tubes were expensive and fragile.

Another man is reported to have seen the device in action, however, and was inspired by it. He was the young Charles Wheatstone, who developed the first generally workable and affordable model twenty years after Ronalds's first demonstration. This was developed into

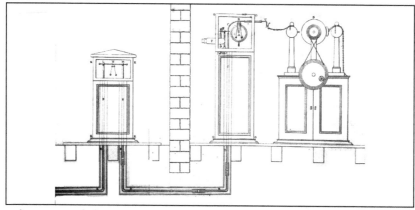

Elements of the Ronald's subterranean electric telegraph, 1816.

the telegraph as we knew it, with modern electricity, Morse code and wires protected by gutta percha, a flexible rubber-like material found in Malaya.

There is no doubt that Ronalds had produced the first electric telegraph, though barely workable by later standards. It predated work by Ampère, Gauss and others by a considerable margin.

Ronalds's interests were much wider than telegraphy. He produced an electric clock and a device (used into the twentieth century) to record air temperature and geomagnetic forces, as well as several other useful devices: the hinged tripod stand for theodolites (and now cameras), a device for identifying the location of a fire and a combined propeller and rudder for boats, among other things.

He collected a large library of books and pamphlets on scientific and technological subjects, which he later presented to the Institution of Electrical Engineers. He was a notable student of meteorology, and in 1843 became the first honorary director and superintendent of the Kew Observatory. He was elected FRS in 1844.

Ronalds retired in 1852 with a pension of £75 per annum, and it was only after much effort by his supporters that in 1870 he was knighted for his telegraphy work. By then he was in Battle, to which he had come to be close to his sister Maria at Telham Court, and was living at St Mary's Villas. Ronalds never married, and in his last years he was cared for by his niece Julia Christiana. She was one of the 499 people who signed the 1866 petition to Parliament in favour of women's franchise.

Polar explorer and
shipwreck hero

✥

Benjamin Leigh Smith
(1828–1913)

A fter the mysterious failure of the Franklin expedition of 1845 the British seem to have had little interest in the Arctic. Leigh Smith was an exception.

He was a great Victorian "gentleman explorer" of the Arctic regions. In the 1870s and 1880s he led five major scientific expeditions, to Svalbard, Jan Mayen, and the newly-discovered Franz Josef Land. He charted much unexplored and undiscovered territory, naming dozens of islands, straits, bays and sounds. He took meticulous records of variations in ocean temperature, invaluable for explorers of the future. He brought back specimens for the Natural History Museum and Kew, and live Polar bears for London Zoo.

Many of his contemporaries believed he would be the first man to reach the North Pole. However, on his fifth expedition his ship, the *Eira*, sank, crushed between ice and land. Leigh Smith kept his entire crew safe through a long Arctic winter, and eventually guided them on a perilous escape to the open sea in their long boats, using damask tablecloths as sails; after travelling for nearly 500 miles they were spotted by a rescue ship, and all returned home alive. Leigh Smith's leadership made him a national hero, but the shipwreck put an end to his Polar career.

"Ben", as he was always known, was born at Petley Lodge, near Whatlington Church. He was the first son and second child of Benjamin Smith, a radical MP from a Unitarian family, and his partner Anne Longden, a milliner whom Smith had met when staying with his sister Fanny Nightingale (mother of Florence) in

Derbyshire. When Anne was found to be pregnant, Smith took her south and set up home for her at Petley Lodge. They had five children together, including the feminist and artist Barbara Leigh Smith Bodichon,* but they never married. Benjamin Smith added "Leigh" to his children's names in order to distinguish them from the vast cohorts of Smith cousins. He made sure they were well educated and well-travelled, but some stigma remained. Ben's illegitimacy was part of the reason why he never received public recognition, such as a knighthood, for his achievements.

After the early death of Anne, Smith moved the family to Pelham Crescent, Hastings. Growing up overlooking the sea gave Ben his taste for maritime adventure. After reading mathematics at Jesus College, Cambridge, Ben read for the bar, but inheriting wealth on the death of his father, plus a legacy from a rich relation, meant that he could abandon his legal career for a life of exploration.

His first voyage was in 1871 when he took the *Sampson*, an 85-ton topsail schooner, to Svalbard. The initial objective was "sport" – Ben was an excellent shot, and he and his companions killed seals, walrus and seabirds in numbers shocking to modern sensibilities. However, he soon developed a serious scientific and geographic interest in the Polar regions, and never again set out with hunting as the principal aim.

On his third expedition, in the steamship *Diana*, Ben went to the rescue of a stranded Swedish expedition, frozen in at Mosselbukta, bringing vital supplies to the starving men and enabling their escape. For this he was awarded the Swedish Royal Order of the Polar Star.

Ben's ambitions increased. He commissioned a vessel of his own; the *Eira*, a 300-ton screw-steamer built at Peterhead to his own specifications. Her first voyage, to Franz Josef Land in 1880, was a great success. Ben explored extensively, mapping, and naming features after friends, colleagues and relations. Names included Nightingale Sound after his cousin Florence, and Cape Leigh Smith; this territory now belongs to Russia, and the cape is "Ostrov Li-Smita". Many remarkable photographs were taken on this expedition. The following year Ben set out again, hoping to push still further north. But the ice conditions were against him, and he and his men

---

* See Chapter 9.

On board the Eira. BLS is the bearded man second from the left; behind him is the young Arthur Conan Doyle, doctor of another ship; Neale is the last on the right.

Courtesy of Hancox archive.

had to bail out quickly as the crushed *Eira* sank just off Cape Flora (named by Ben after a Smith cousin).

The men saved what they could from the sinking ship, including ammunition, tinned food, Bob the dog, the cat, a canary, a musical box, plenty of champagne, and the all-important table cloths. They built a shelter in which they survived nine months of Arctic winter, shooting bears and birds to eat. Ben timetabled each day with strict discipline, ably assisted by his ship's doctor, Dr Neale.* The survival of every single crew member is testimony to their skills.

When the ice started to break up, in June 1882, they took to the boats they had saved, and set off. After six weeks at sea, they came within hailing distance of the rescue party that had set out in search of them. All were returned safely to Aberdeen, including Bob the dog.

---

* Neale was to give the name Eira to his daughter.

Ben returned to find himself a celebrity, but he shied away, dreading publicity, he said, "worse than ice". This reserve, together with his "outsider" status as a Dissenter and as illegitimate, and his failure to write up fully the results of his expeditions, combined to mean that he is far less well known to Polar history than his achievements deserve.

Ben owned property in the Battle region including Mountfield Park Farm, Glottenham Manor (now a care home), and Brown's farmhouse, near Robertsbridge. After his sister Barbara's death he inherited her house, Scalands Gate, between Robertsbridge and Brightling. He took a great interest in farming, especially hop growing (he issued his own hop tokens) and in the management of his estates. A wealthy bachelor, he dismayed most of his family by marrying Charlotte Sellars, a beautiful, penniless orphan, when he was 60 and she was 19. The couple had two sons, but eventually separated.

Ben developed dementia in his old age; Charlotte continued to live at Scalands, but Ben was housed in Hampstead, looked after by two attendants and supervised by his old friend and Polar colleague Dr Neale. Ben died in January 1913 and was buried at Brightling, his grave marked by a traditional wooden Sussex gravemarker. His sister Barbara's grave lies alongside.

In 2017, the wreck of the *Eira* was found by a Russian scientific expeditionary ship, the *Alter Ego*. Some exploratory diving has been carried out, and more investigation is planned.

8
Health and the professions

All market towns have their professionals – lawyers, doctors, vets and chemists. Battle is no different, having had them probably since before monks left the Abbey in 1538. Some were indeed remarkable people worthy of notice to our and later generations.

The man who saved many lives

❧❧

Edward Cresy
(1792–1858)

There is a traditional picture of the old-time countryside as one of peaceful and healthy people living in cottages that may have been primitive but were decent homes in which to bring up children and pass long lives. In some small places this was more true than in others, but in the market towns there was a rather different picture: overcrowding, a lack of effective sewerage and occasional outbreaks of disease that could have been prevented. In some of them – Battle being a good example, for it stands on a ridge – there was also a water supply problem.

Water was crucial to improvement, not only because contaminated water brought disease, but also because without it, houses and persons couldn't be kept properly clean and sewage, a main contaminant, couldn't be efficiently removed. Every house needed effective cleaning agents that would act against infestations of flies with their maggots, cockroaches and body lice – the latter sometimes carrying the Rickettsia bacteria causing the lethal infection typhus.

Battle was unusually early in making use of the opportunities offered by the 1848 Public Health Act. Very soon after the General Board of Health's first announcements, fifty local rate-payers of Battle – the required minimum – petitioned it. Battle had all the problems that a market town might have. Disease there was common, often leading to an early death. There was no running water, the wells were frequently contaminated, and there was no effective sewerage system. The churchyard was (at times literally) overflowing. Houses were often badly ventilated and sometimes overrun with animal effluent. What is now Lewinscroft in Mount Street had 48 inhabitants and its condition was to cause argument into the twentieth century. These problems were known and very often accepted ('that's life', people must have said), but the fifty ratepayers must have been just waiting their chance.

Cresy was the visiting inspector. He was a Chartered Engineer who had turned his attention to the problems of public health. He arrived at Battle in June 1850. His report must have saved many lives in the years to come.

He visited only the urban part of town, not the whole parish. Conditions there were very far from satisfactory, and Cresy pulled no punches. It was a full report, of some 28 pages, and it told a miserable tale. It was published on 24 December 1850, and comments were invited.

With the exception of one house on Battle Hill, the population obtained its water from collected roof water or from wells or pools that were often polluted. Sewage went into cesspools that sometimes overflowed and were almost always foul-smelling. There were numerous slaughterhouses and piggeries, the effluent from which was hard to control and sometimes flowed into houses. Some houses were badly ventilated and damp. Diseases such as typhoid and typhus were common. Conditions in the churchyard were such as to require a complete cessation of burials there.

In Lower Lake there was a house with a privy and pigsties at the rear, at a higher level, and their overflow ran across the house floor. What is now the Pilgrims' Rest (which he called the Almonry) next to the Abbey was occupied by several tenants. He wrote:

> The first family is Frank Butler's, behind which are two cottages, weather-boarded on the outside, ... badly ventilated, there being no windows in the rear. Pigsties and open cesspools close to the houses, discharging by fetid ditches into the George Meadow, are much complained of from the smells which arise.

> The Almonry is an old timbered house, covered with tiles, and under that part of the roof which is in the occupation of James Jenner, several pigs are kept; and where Ashton Tongs has his rooms, both pigs and privy are highly offensive. The three families who reside here ... have all had fever ... how different the state of this old mansion when occupied by the steward of the wealthy

Abbey, placed in the midst of a well-cultivated garden, occupied by one family, and surrounded by a healthy atmosphere, instead of the pollution which now lies at the very threshold.

Arrangements for the disposal of waste matter could not be called a system. On part of the High Street there was a pipe that ran under some of the houses and then opened into the field behind, finally into Marley Stream and so down to the river Brede. At the north end of the High Street there was nothing: waste material ran across the High Street and down to the Asten Stream; not for nothing was Shytteborne Lane so called (now bowdlerised into Western Avenue). On the south-west side these unpleasant materials went into cess pits, which sometimes overflowed, and then down to the site of the cricket ground and also into the Asten Stream. Lower Lake's waste ran down the road and gardens to the stream at the foot of the hill. As so often people tolerated the dangers and the smells: at least one was inclined to resist official intervention because she made money by selling the material from her dungheaps.

Comments provided more first-hand evidence of preventable disease, and there was no delay in getting things done. In May 1851 the General Board authorised the creation of a local urban sanitary board and the ratepayers established it within two months, on the back of a loan of £1,800 from the County Fire Office.

The obvious first point of action was to supply water, for without it the sewerage system couldn't start. A reservoir was promptly built at the top of Caldbec Hill and water pumped up to it from a well in the field below that had housed the barracks closed in 1815.

The new sewerage system came into being in 1854 and was effective. No figures are available for the reduction in disease but it must have been noticeable.

The matter of the cemetery, however, was controversial. The Dean insisted that there was room in the churchyard for the 40 or so burials a year. It had been used since about 1100, which suggests an unseen underground population of perhaps 20,000, so tending to cast doubt on the Dean's view. The General Board issued notices of closure for that burial ground and those of the two dissenting chapels at the other end of the town. The vestry seems to have regarded

PUBLIC HEALTH ACT,

(11 & 12 Vict., Cap. 63.)

REPORT

TO THE

GENERAL BOARD OF HEALTH

ON A

PRELIMINARY INQUIRY

INTO THE SEWERAGE, DRAINAGE, AND SUPPLY OF
WATER, AND THE SANITARY CONDITION
OF THE INHABITANTS

OF THE TOWN OF

BATTLE,

IN THE COUNTY OF SUSSEX.

By EDWARD CRESY, Esq. C.E.,
SUPERINTENDING INSPECTOR.

LONDON.

PRINTED BY W. CLOWES & SONS, STAMFORD STREET
FOR HER MAJESTY'S STATIONERY OFFICE.

1850

**Cover page of Cresy's report, soon to be accepted by the
General Board of Health**

the matter as unnecessary and certainly not urgent. In 1855, after a
Government order not to bury any more bodies in the churchyard,
a corpse awaiting burial lay in the church for some time because the
Dean would be fined £10 for proceeding in the usual way. It was
claimed by the vestry that there was:

ground vacant and fit for interment in single or separate graves for 511 bodies – that there was ground that had not been disturbed for twenty-five years fit for interment in single and separate graves for 440 bodies – and that there was ground in which, during the last twenty-five years, 820 bodies have been interred...

A public meeting in 1851 was told by the vestry that the noxious effluent from the churchyard, to which Cresy had drawn attention, could be removed by better drainage. It was not until 1862 that after much further pressure a new cemetery opened off Marley Lane; no-one was to be buried elsewhere. The Burials Board remained part of the ecclesiastical establishment until 1934.

The doctor who trapped a murderer

❧❧

Henry Montagu Champneys
(1818–1895)

One Battle doctor had been involved in a famous murder, though on the right side of things and before he came to live and work at Battle. This was Champneys, who practised at Battle with the Watts family, and he must have been the successor to the disgraced Charles West Roberts in the winter of 1861/62. He had married Catherine Laurence of Battle in 1851, and three of their children were born in the town. The 1861 census records him as living at Slough.

Champneys was well-known at one point because of his action in a famous murder case – that of Sarah Hart by John Tawell in 1845.

He was Sarah Hart's doctor and was called to the dying woman. He detected poisoning; on being given the description of the man who had fled the house for the railway station, he ran after him, At the station he found that the suspected murderer had just left for London so he caused a description to be sent by telegraph to Paddington station. Tawell was met by police when his train arrived.

Champneys gave evidence to both the coroner and to the trial court that he had identified prussic acid (hydrocyanide) in Sarah Hart's stomach. Tawell was found guilty and executed at Aylesbury. Publicity given to the then new telegraph was enormous and must have contributed to its rapid spread.

He did not stay at Battle long, leaving for Penge in 1867.

The solicitor who ran a town

❧❦

William Augustus Raper
(1845–1940)

Raper is probably the one solicitor above all others who deserves commemoration. His father was to become medical officer of health for Portsmouth, and he arrived at Battle in 1870, replacing the just-deceased Frederick Ellman in the practice of that name based at 1 Upper Lake. For a short time he was partner with Ellman's son Henry but soon worked on his own, though the name Ellman remained in the partnership well into the next century.

The young lawyer made his name in the Ashdown Forest case of 1876–82. This began when a commoner of the forest ordered his servant to cut bracken and other material from it. An agent of the landowner, Earl de la Warr, asked him to desist, and he refused. De la Warr therefore brought a case to enforce what he believed (or hoped) were his rights. The commoner, however, was not only a barrister but also Deputy Lieutenant of Sussex, and not a man to be frightened. He engaged Raper, who meticulously assembled copious evidence, both local and legal, to support the rights of the commoners, and after a long time the commoners won the case. It was a legal landmark.

By 1881 Raper had begun his long residence at 12/13 Upper Lake, with which he incorporated 14 and 15 as his family increased. The whole building was until recently better known as Pyke House, named after a later owner, and it is now a boarding house for Claremont School. Augustus and his wife had four sons and four daughters, which helps to explain the need for enlargement. The direct Raper connection with Battle seems now to have been lost, though a grandson, also William Augustus (1911–1987), served as a partner of the practice for some years.

The records show that Raper was held in the highest regard, and

MR WILLIAM AUGUSTUS RAPER

**William Augustus Raper, *The Sussex County Magazine,*
April 1926**

rightly so. Much of Battle's development in the early years of self-government was guided by him. He played so large a part in public life, and presumably with his family, that one is led to wonder how much time was left for the law.

From 1875 Raper was a member of the sanitary authority set up in 1851, the body first intended to provide the town with running water and sewage disposal but accruing more powers as time went on. By 1894 he was its chairman; when the Urban District Council succeeded it under the 1894 Local Government Act, he was the natural choice to chair it. He did so until 1919 – as the Urban

District was to be abolished in 1934 he was chairman for more than half its busy and useful life. He was also a county councillor and a churchwarden and a member of the Burials Board. For long periods he was clerk of the Commissioners of Income and Assessed Taxes (this was before PAYE), and clerk and treasurer of the combined Battle charities.

His standing was so high that on his seventieth birthday the bells of St Mary's rang specially for him. He was also an active member of the Sussex Archaeological Society and of the local Conservative Party and chairman of the (rather unpopular) gas company.

He had misfortunes with three of his four sons. The eldest, William, was a naval surgeon who died on Malta in 1904 (there is a plaque to his memory in St Mary's Church), and the next brother Henry, a solicitor like his father, had died in 1899. Then came Robert, killed in the 1914–18 war. The last, Godfrey, also served in that war.

Robert had joined the territorial battalion of the Royal Sussex in 1896, and had been posted to garrison duty at Shorncliffe during the Boer War; he had been promoted Captain in 1908. He was therefore subject to immediate call-up in 1914, and applied for a commission in the Royal Sussex. There followed a delay, and such was his enthusiasm that he decided to find another regiment, in this case the South Staffordshires. By then he had married and had started a family. He and his wife were to have three children before he died, and one followed posthumously. They lived at Richards Hill, a large Victorian house on the south side of Powdermill Lane, shortly west of the entry to what is now the Powder Mills hotel.

Robert died in 1916, on the second day of the battle of the Somme. He had led his men into Fricourt, and then pushed northwards until he was killed in action. He is now buried in the Bray Road Military Cemetery just outside Fricourt, and the longest road in Fricourt bears his name. In his memory his brother Godfrey erected a chapel there that stands today.

After his death the Dean of Battle gave a tribute to him on Sunday, 9 July, speaking of "a life without reproach crowned by a death of heroic self-sacrifice". Later it was reported that the Commander-in-Chief, Sir Douglas Haig, had proposed special mention not only of Robert but also of his brother Godfrey, and he did so again at the

At Fricourt, département of the Somme.
Photo: Neil Clephane-Cameron, 2016.

end of the war. It was also reported that at the beginning of the war Godfrey had returned to the UK 'to do his bit for the empire', having handed over the management of his interests in Colorado to a friend.

After the war Augustus was reducing his commitments to his practice as well as to local government and Reginald Fovargue became a partner in 1922, soon marrying Robert's widow. The law practice was then named Raper and Fovargue, a name that it retained until the Heringtons merger of 1986.

The Irish doctor and writer

Sir Norman Moore, Bt
(1847–1922)

Moore was a remarkable man, and not just as a doctor. After a long career at St Bartholomew's Hospital he became President of the Royal College of Physicians, but his interests extended beyond medicine; he was a historian, naturalist, linguist, bibliophile, antiquarian, and proponent of Irish culture. He lived at Whatlington, worshipped at Battle and was buried at Sedlescombe.

Moore's father, Robert Ross Rowan Moore, was a radical barrister from Dublin, active in the Anti-Corn Law League; his mother, Rebecca Fisher, was a Quaker from Limerick. Norman never knew his father, for by the time of the birth he had left Rebecca for another woman. This surely cannot have been unexpected. Rowan's political colleague John Bright remarked "for God's sake keep Moore off our platforms, I do not think there is any man in either party who he has not cuckolded".

Norman Moore was brought up in Higher Broughton, Manchester, by his mother. He was the only child of a single parent. Rebecca was an active feminist who would sign the petition for female suffrage presented to Parliament in 1866. Twenty-two years earlier, Rowan Moore had stood (unsuccessfully) for Parliament at Hastings; this had resulted in a friendship with Barbara Leigh Smith, later Bodichon, a prime mover of the suffrage petition. Norman was destined to marry two of Barbara's nieces, first Amy Leigh Smith, then Milicent Ludlow.

Norman was educated at a boarding school in Lancaster run by William Herford, a liberal Unitarian. The boys were taken on adventurous climbing expeditions, giving Norman a life-long taste

Sir Norman Moore,
courtesy of the Hancox archive

for exploration. At this enlightened school he was allowed to develop his interests in birdwatching, falconry and botany. However, money was tight, and at the age of thirteen he was obliged to leave. He found a job in a cotton warehouse in Manchester, earning sixteen shillings a month. After work, he attended evening classes at Owens College, and eventually won a scholarship to St Catharine's College, Cambridge, to read natural sciences.

By then, he had been befriended by the remarkable explorer and naturalist Charles Waterton, author of *Wanderings in South America*. Aged 16, Norman had walked 43 miles to visit Waterton's collection of stuffed birds and animals at Walton Hall, near Wakefield. He fell into conversation with the elderly Waterton, and thereafter was a frequent guest. Walton Hall was the first nature reserve in the country; Waterton built a wall round the estate and decreed that no shot could be fired within this wall. Waterton's generosity to his young protégé extended to his offering Norman the family's

First Folio Shakespeare, which – unfortunately – Norman politely declined!

Charles Waterton was a teetotaller and a Roman Catholic. Norman, who was deeply influenced by him, followed suit, though he did not convert to Catholicism until he was in his fifties. Waterton died following an accident; Norman, who was with him at the time, wrote an account.

After Cambridge he pursued his medical career at St Bartholomew's in London. Bart's did not charge fees, and so was of great value to the many poor of London. Norman's casebooks, describing treatment of patients, are of great interest. He wrote a definitive history of Bart's, published in 1918. In the same year he became President of the Royal College of Physicians, and in 1919 he was made a baronet.

Norman published medical textbooks and papers. He also contributed 469 articles to the *Dictionary of National Biography*, which he had been instrumental in setting up. Many of his subjects were Irish saints; though he never lived in Ireland, Norman identified strongly as Irish, and walked the length and breadth of the island, starting at the age of 15 when he walked 120 miles from Dublin to Limerick, sleeping in the open or as the guest of cottagers. He had a huge circle of friends, ranging from Irish labourers met on his walking tours to eminent Victorians and Edwardians including Charles Darwin, Henry James, General Sir Evelyn Wood, Hilaire Belloc and Leslie Stephen. Thousands of the letters he wrote and received have been preserved. He was Darwin's doctor, and wrote his death certificate.

Norman's first marriage was opposed by his wife Amy's family, who regarded him as a penniless Irishman. However, opposition was overcome. The marriage was happy and produced three children – Alan, who served as a Naval surgeon during the First World War and became a hard-working and effective medical officer of health when the new Battle Rural District came into being in 1934, Ethne, an artist who married a Hertfordshire squire, and Gillachrist ('servant of Christ' in Irish), a 2nd Lieutenant in the Royal Sussex Regiment who was killed at the first Battle of Ypres.

After Amy's early death in 1901 from tuberculosis, Norman married her cousin Milicent Ludlow. Milicent owned Hancox in

Whatlington; this became the family home (and is now occupied by Norman's great-grand daughter and her family). The Battle area was second only to Ireland in Norman's affections. He worshipped at the Catholic church in Mount Street and took an active part in local life.

Norman never fully recovered from the shock of Gillachrist's death; his diaries are testament to his great grief. He was involved in war work, including hearing a total of nine hundred petitions from men applying for war pensions on the grounds of physical or mental ill health, but his own health began to decline. He died at Hancox in November 1922, and was buried, according to Catholic rites, in the churchyard at Sedlescombe. A large number of distinguished people attended.

The doctor who never took a holiday

❦

George Kendall
(1859–1932)

Kendall was the third doctor of outstanding memory. He was at 69/70 High Street; after the First World War he moved to 36 High Street, where he would remain until his retirement in 1928; it is still a surgery.

Kendall's father, a Yorkshireman, was a pharmaceutical chemist living at Kennington, in the vestry (later borough), of Lambeth which is where Kendall was born. He qualified as a physician in 1884 – MRCS (England) and LRCP (London); Battle may have been both his first and last practice. He was also surgeon to the Battle workhouse for a time, when the two doctors concerned went to the war.

A source states:

> Before the introduction of the National Health Service patients paid their GP for any necessary treatment. Many could not afford it but Dr Kendall, who was united in his devotion to his patients, refused to charge anyone who, he thought, would have difficulty paying.
>
> He would come out at any time of day or night in his pony and trap, driven by his coachman Mr Charles Turner (later his chauffeur). Any medicines he prescribed he either brought himself, or sent, often by an old man called Edwards, who would walk with his basket from the High Street in Battle, sometimes miles to an outlying village.

He appears to have been a modest man: when nominated to be Medical Officer of Health in 1896 he declined, in favour of another

Kendall and his wife Ada
Photo: Trevor Wayne, courtesy of Battle Museum

doctor whom he felt to be better-qualified. He was highly regarded by the local population, and the Museum has a statement attesting to this (*see overleaf*).

When the war ended Kendall was one of those prominent in seeking a constructive war memorial for the town rather than just a carved list, and the local council agreed to support his proposal for a nursing home; but the money could not be raised. Enthusiasm fell away after the Dean erected his memorial in the churchyard of St Mary's. Kendall was to return to Battle to be buried in the town cemetery.

At his farewell on retirement it was stated that the only times that he had left his practice were for his honeymoon and when he was unwell, so only twice and for short times.

Ada died at Battle in 1911 and his mother in 1914, also at Battle; his nephew Robert, who had lived at Battle, died of wounds received in action in 1916. John, another nephew, joined his practice after war service and left it after his uncle retired. George was not a rich man and the fund collected for him was enough to purchase a freehold residence in King's Drive, Eastbourne.

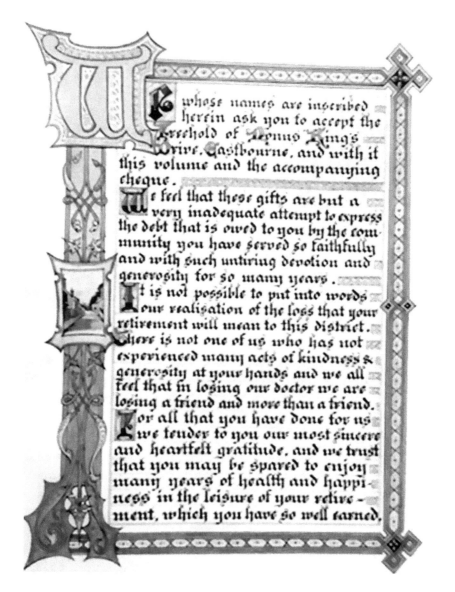

We whose names are inscribed herein ask you to accept the freehold of Aepuns King's Drive, Eastbourne, and with it this volume and the accompanying cheque.

We feel that these gifts are but a very inadequate attempt to express the debt that is owed to you by the community you have served so faithfully and with such untiring devotion and generosity for so many years.

It is not possible to put into words our realisation of the loss that your retirement will mean to this district. There is not one of us who has not experienced many acts of kindness & generosity at your hands and we all feel that in losing our doctor we are losing a friend and more than a friend.

For all that you have done for us we tender to you our most sincere and heartfelt gratitude, and we trust that you may be spared to enjoy many years of health and happiness in the leisure of your retirement, which you have so well earned,

Testament to George Kendall
Photo: Trevor Wayne, courtesy of Battle Museum

144

9
Politics

❦

The Battle area has nearly always been politically quiet and its MPs little known outside the area. But four people stand out.

Rural Rides and Captain Swing

❦

William Cobbett
(1763–1835)

Cobbett was a campaigner on all kinds of issues, not necessarily consistent in his support or opposition except for two: the importance of agriculture and the problem of corruption in public office. He was an able writer and speaker, capable of rousing people in his support and simultaneously angering his enemies. His connection with Battle arose from his two visits, and in particular that as the Swing 'riots' were just beginning, which led to his unsuccessful prosecution for seditious libel.

He was the son of a farmer/publican of Farnham, growing up in an agricultural world threatened by enclosures – the private Acts of Parliament by which already established landlords took over common land to which every citizen had had rights to wood and crops and to pasture for their sheep and other animals.

Agriculture was to face worse threats later. By 1830, on his second visit to Battle, the situation was serious. Farmers and their labourers were even more poorly paid than before, thanks largely to the Corn Law of 1815 that protected grain producers from competition from abroad. Importers would have to pay £4 per quarter until domestic prices reached that level. This meant that the price of grain rose high (but carefully never reaching £4), with increased profits to landlords and large farmers but much higher prices for animal feeds, flour and other grain products. Cobbett's book, *Rural Rides,* was a good, if polemic, description of the agricultural situation, to which he had pointed in an address at Battle in 1822 to an audience of about 300 people.

By 1830 things had deteriorated. Cobbett came at the very beginning of the disturbances known as the 'Swing riots'. The 'Swing' comes from an almost certainly mythical person allegedly organising the disturbances. There are theories about him but he remains a mystery. Various copies of threats to barns and crops survive in that name. The 'riots' were not as we would now understand the word: certainly people gathered and looked menacing, but in Battle at least there was no violence and no looting. The actions prompting the term were almost all arson: the burning of barns and hayricks. They never included shops and houses, often with deaths, that characterised some of the Reform riots of 1831.

On 16 October 1830 Cobbett addressed a large group of people at Battle, from a platform erected by local associates. The audience here, as in 1822, was drawn from a wide area and would have been conscious of the major disturbances already taking place in Kent. Cobbett wanted prosperity in the countryside, wages to rise and the end of the Corn Laws, and (according to his version) he counselled against violence.

That was not good enough for the Government of the day, perhaps the most reactionary in the last three centuries but about to collapse. It was early in November that violence took place, and two labourers (Edmund Bushby and Thomas Goodman) were charged and sentenced to death, arson then being a capital offence. The government saw that if one of these men could give evidence of incitement against Cobbett they could reprieve him and prosecute the speaker. Goodman had been at the lecture and was clearly the officials' target.

Goodman was promised his life if he made the right statement. How many of us would refuse? But fatally for the authorities it took three attempts to get the statement right for them. Part of the final version read:

> ... he had a great deal of discussion about the states of the people and the country, telling that they were verrey much impose upon and he would tell them how to get the better of it or they would soon be starved. He said it would be verrey Proper for every man to keep a gun in his house especially young men and that they might prepare themselves in readdyness to go with him When he called on them and he would show them the way to get their rights and liberals(liberties) and he said that the Farmers must expect there

would be Firs [fires] in susex and in Battel as well as other Places and is conversation was all as sutch to inflame Peopels minds , they thinking that he would be A friend to them which made a very great imprision upon me and so inflame my mine and I from that time was determined to set stacks on fire and soon afterwards there was three firs in Battle and that same night the last fire was at the Corsbarn ..

Goodman was promptly transported to Australia, though Bushby (who came from near Littlehampton) was hanged. Cobbett went rather further in another article in his *Political Register*, drawing a connection between the rioting and arson and the campaign to increase wages.

The new government of 1830 continued the prosecution and it was a mighty failure. Not only did Cobbett have behind him a petition signed by 103 farmers, craftsmen and labourers stating that he had not incited violence, but it became clear that Goodman's evidence was the last of three versions. This strongly suggested that the first two had been found insufficient by the prosecution and, as his life was under threat, Goodman would have complied with their requests for something that might convince a jury.

The case came to trial in July 1831, and Cobbett tried to call as witnesses several members of the Cabinet to demonstrate their false motives. Only the Home Secretary appeared, and the judge ruled that he should not give evidence. In the end the jury were divided and the case was dropped. This was the last of several attempts to imprison him or worse, only one of which had been successful.

The other issue was corruption. It used to be hard for us to imagine the level of corruption among ministers and MPs. Even now it may be unlikely to reach quite its level in the early nineteenth century. It had Cobbett as its loudest enemy.

He had first met corruption when serving in the army, from 1791. He found that the quarter-master general was keeping food back and selling it for his own gain, and that officers were declaring that they had more men than they did, thereby pocketing the wages of non-existent troops. Cobbett tried to prove this but the evidence disappeared and he withdrew the case. As he was still a soldier he feared the worst and fled first to France and then to the USA, where

From *Rural Rides*, by William Cobbett
Courtesy of Project Gutenberg

he carried on his combative attitude and founded his *Political Register*.

On his return as a civilian he found further corruption, at first in an MP who had been given a lucrative sinecure, thus being paid for doing nothing but guaranteeing his support for the government; this was small business. Cobbett later found that the Speaker of the

Commons, whose salary was £6,000, also had a government position in Ireland worth £15,000. The Chancellor of the Exchequer had a salary of £2,600 but held a second Cabinet post and one at the Royal Mint, each for £4,525. Using the retail price index would give the Speaker an annual income from public sources of more than £1,640,00 in 2019 and the Chancellor a little under a million. No wonder Cobbett argued strongly for Parliamentary reform.

He died only five years after leaving Battle. During that short period he retained a distant connection through his secretary James Gutsell, who had been instrumental in setting up the 1830 meeting and who was to die only very shortly after Cobbett. Cobbett's son James was a prominent Chartist for a short time.

The Corn Laws ended in 1846 in a political battle that split the Tory Party.

The only Cabinet minister

⚛⚛⚛

John George Dodson
(1825–1897)

Dodson was not only the only local MP known to have been in the Cabinet but also effectively the last non-Conservative to represent the Battle area in Parliament.[*]

John Dodson, after James Tissot, in *Vanity Fair* 1871

Not principally of a landowning family, he was the son of a judge, once MP for Rye, who married the daughter of a well-known chemist and physician.

Dodson was educated at Eton and Oxford and then went to

---

[*] Actually the last was C F Hutchinson, who won a by-election in 1903, but lasted only to late 1905.

the Bar. His local connections were that his family was based at Hurstpierpoint and that he married a grand-daughter of Thomas Kemp, who developed much of Brighton and is commemorated in the name Kemptown.

Dodson first contested the Eastern Sussex constituency in 1852 and was elected in 1857, holding the seat until 1874. By then his electoral position looked shaky and he moved to be MP for Chester and later for Scarborough. In 1865–72 he was Chairman of Ways and Means in the Commons and in 1873–74 Financial Secretary to the Treasury, but then the Government fell.

From 1874 to 1876 he chaired the Public Accounts Committee. The Liberals returned to government in 1880 and he became President of the Local Government Board and in 1882–84 Chancellor of the Duchy of Lancaster. He became the first Lord Monk Bretton in this last year. In 1889 he became the first chairman of the new East Sussex County Council.

Dodson was a Liberal and a strong supporter of Gladstone until the Irish Home Rule crisis of 1886. This split his party, and a large number left it to form the Liberal Unionists; Dodson was among them. Monk Bretton is near Barnsley in the West Riding, which seems an odd connection; he had inherited some land there from his mother.

The great feminist campaigner

❧

Barbara Bodichon
(1827–1891)

B arbara Leigh Smith Bodichon is in this chapter because of
her contribution to the women's fight for equality; she was
also a successful landscape artist, exhibiting in London and
elsewhere. It may be a significant indication of the age that when
she died her obituary in *The Times* mentioned her art but not her
contributions to education or to women's rights.

Barbara Leigh Bodichon
Courtesy of the Hancox Archive

The noise made later in respect of the equal Parliamentary vote,
achieved more or less fully only in 1928, tends to blot out the
earlier campaigns for equality. Yet 1928 was only one point in the

slow process of establishing gender equality, albeit one of the most important ones. It can be argued that without earlier changes and the growth of women's education nothing much would have happened. Barbara Bodichon was instrumental in having them made.

The position of women in the early nineteenth century was to our eyes intolerable, but it was as it always had been. There had been improvements driven by the women themselves, almost entirely those with some wealth, as the growing number of female authors and scientists showed. But in law they still had few rights. Unless prior agreement had been made, a bride surrendered any wealth to her husband; divorce was legally more difficult for women than for men, involving considerable expense, and few had money; and they had no right to vote.

Barbara Bodichon was one of the earliest open campaigners for women's rights. She had been born at Petley Lodge, Whatlington, the illegitimate daughter of Benjamin Smith MP. The Smiths were a large, prosperous and influential Unitarian family; Florence Nightingale was Barbara's first cousin. Her mother, Anne Longden, was a working-class woman from Derbyshire. Benjamin never married her, but he treated her as his wife and was an active father to their five children. He insisted on educating his three daughters to the same level as his two sons.

Benjamin Smith owned property in Hastings, Westfield, Mountfield and Robertsbridge as well as Whatlington. After Anne Longden's early death, he moved the children to the recently-built Pelham Crescent in Hastings; here Barbara grew up. She retained links to the Battle area for the rest of her life, building herself a house, Scalands Gate, between Robertsbridge and Brightling; it was modelled on a Saxon manor house, and it was decorated with a frieze of the Bayeux Tapestry. She entertained many guests at Scalands, including, amongst many others, fellow artists such as Rossetti and William Morris, the novelist George Eliot, the suffragist campaigner Millicent Fawcett, Elizabeth Blackwell, the pioneering woman doctor, and the great plantswoman Gertrude Jekyll, who helped Barbara create a wild garden at Scalands. The guests painted their names on the bricks surrounding the big fireplace – this was Barbara's 'Visitors' Book'.

Her work started early, in the belief that women's education was crucial to their winning more significant acceptance. Her father gave her the title-deeds to an experimental infant school he had founded in Vincent Square, Westminster. She went on to found the socially and educationally radical Portman Hall School. In 1866, with Emily Davies, she founded the first university college for women, which became Girton College, Cambridge. Her action meant that women could now take courses and examinations at the university – though, true to ancient form, Cambridge did not actually award them degrees until 1949.

Barbara initiated the 'Langham Place Group', an all-female pressure group which included the Married Women's Property Committee. In 1854, Barbara published *A Brief Summary in Plain Language of the most important Laws concerning Women*. This became an action list for campaigners.

By the early nineteenth century there had been a tiny crack in the political establishment, which very quickly closed. In 1832 Henry 'Orator' Hunt, the star of Peterloo, presented to Parliament a petition from Mary Smith, a Yorkshire woman who paid taxes and obeyed the law but was not entitled to vote. Needless to say it did not succeed, and the Reform Act of that year was the first move formally and specifically to ban women from voting.

Smith and Hunt were properly addressing the major problem. Without Parliamentary rights, the law would take longer to change in all the other areas where women's rights were suppressed. These included all the professions, with an unintended gap in medicine where, whoever drafted the Royal Charter of the Society of Apothecaries, forgot to limit its licensing role to benefit only men, thus allowing Elizabeth Garrett Anderson to become the first female doctor to qualify in the UK in 1865. (Much later she was the first woman mayor in England, too).

Barbara was a founder of the Women's Suffrage Committee, which spread across the country. In 1866 she was one of those who managed the petition to Parliament to be presented by John Stuart Mill in an attempt to have women included in the second Reform Act then under discussion: where the Bill used the word men as voters the proposal was to use persons. 1499 signatures were listed, including that of the physicist Mary Somerville, who signed from La Spezia in Italy, along with two female relatives there (the final figure reported was 1521, which suggests 22 further, late, additions). Mill had adopted women's suffrage and women's representation in Parliament as a cause.

But a matter noted by the committee on the Bill was that the great majority of signatures were not on the main document but were pasted on to it; this must have given reason, or excuse, for it to be taken less credibly. Predictably, the vote in the Commons attracted only 73 votes and it lost, but the creation of an active pressure group for women's votes, the Kensington Society, in which Barbara played a leading role, was an enduring achievement.

It seems likely that in obtaining support for the petition she had taken the initiative in the Battle area, though it may be that she had persuaded another person to do so. Unfortunately there were no signatures from the villages around Battle: it is unlikely that they were not sought, but any sympathetic individuals may have been isolated and faced local opposition or even derision.

It is a tribute to Barbara's connections with Sussex that she canvassed 53 people in the county and that there were seventeen Battle signatories to the petition, a large figure for such a small town. A similar statistical distortion took place in Suffolk, where the small town of Aldeburgh provided 19, presumably collected by the Garrett sisters who were to play notable roles in the long-running campaign for equality. (Birmingham provided three signatures).

The notice of the petition, as reported in its prefatory document, is headed by three names: Barbara L.S. Bodichon, Clementia Taylor (a vigorous campaigner for better education for all) and Emily Davies. The 1866 signatories from Battle were, with details as far as we know:

Name	Age	Status
Avery, Sarah	Uncertain	
Blackman, Mary Ann	21	Single, cook
Burgess, Ann	44	Single, stationer
Burgess, Caroline	58	Wife of draper
Burgess, Ellen	31	Single, daughter of draper
Chettle, Leah	44	Wife of watchmaker
Dench, Mary Ann	47	Single, assistant stationer

Edwards, Philadelphia	28	Single, daughter of ironmonger
Edwards, Elizabeth	43	Wife of ironmonger
Fisher, Rebecca	Uncertain	
Ronalds, Julia	37	Single, niece of Telham Court owner
Russell, Mary Ann	Uncertain	
Slatter, Jane	51	Single, sister of grocer
Ticehurst, Emily	21	Single, daughter of postmaster
Ticehurst, Elizabeth	15	Single, daughter of postmaster
Weller, Caroline	64	Wife of saddler, surveyor, coal merchant
Weller, Emily	42	Single, daughter of above

We know little more about the women above except that some, perhaps most if not all, were dissenting Protestants and none except Julia Ronalds were connected to major landowners.

The petition was effectively the beginning of organised pressure for equality. It had a slow but definite effect. Education boards set up in and after 1870 could include women. One of the first two women to be elected to the new London County Council in 1889 was Jane Cobden, also from Sussex, though the courts ruled against female participation shortly afterwards. Women had increasing local rights to vote in 1894 (urban and rural district councils) and in 1907 (boroughs and counties). These rights were rarely exactly those of men but they were a start.

Barbara Bodichon never gave up easily. She had been an organiser of the 1854 petition to the House of Lords, with some 26,000 signatures, proposing what became the Married Women's Property Act. It passed its first and second readings in the Commons in 1857 but got no further at that stage. A limited Act was passed in 1870, allowing women to keep any earnings they had. By the time that the major Act was passed in 1882 she was largely paralysed after a stroke and so had to withdraw from active campaigning. That Act established a wife's right to retain any property brought to her marriage.

In 1857 Barbara married Eugène Bodichon, a Breton doctor working in Algeria. The couple divided their time between Algeria, where Barbara created a wonderful garden, London and

Barbara Bodichon by Samuel Lawrence, 1880
Courtesy of the Hancox archive

Robertsbridge. To her sorrow, the marriage was childless. After her first stroke in 1877 she travelled less and spent most of her time at Scalands Gate, where she died.

The final victory for the franchise was achieved less by direct and continuing pressure for it – though that was certainly there – but by an accretion of rights other than the franchise itself.

The campaigning abolitionist

༄

Guy Hayler
(1850–1943)

The Battle-born Hayler* was a noted campaigner for the prohibition of alcohol for recreational consumption. He was also an active Freemason, achieving the rank of Master Mason in 1885, and Grand Counsellor of the Grand Lodge of Good Templars.

In the twenty-first century we're much more concerned with drugs other than alcohol, though both can lead to serious health problems; and drugs, being illegal, offer more or less unlimited opportunities for crime and its associated violence, exactly like illegal alcohol during American prohibition. There remain campaigns against both, though not now generally associated with dissenting religion and radical politics.

This was not so in the nineteenth century, when drugs were legal but alcohol was the universal and identifiable curse. The licensing of premises to sell alcoholic beverages dates back to 1552, and was based on the need to ensure standards and the collection of taxes. Even under Cromwell's Protectorate, when almost every form of enjoyment was banned there was no attempt to impose controls on alcohol.

In the following century the enemy was not beer but gin, and various Acts of Parliament sought to diminish its role in the social disorders famously depicted by William Hogarth. Far from banning drinking, after largely unsuccessful attempts to control gin the aim became to divert people to less damaging fluids. In 1830 the

---

* References to the family source and other information, have been kindly provided by a descendant, Shirley Hare, from her book *The Hayler Family & Bulmer* (1986).

Beerhouse Act allowed people to sell beer but not spirits. Someone could now sell beer without the prior agreement of the local justices, simply on payment of an annual fee.

The movement towards total abstinence seems to have begun in about 1820, and it made rapid inroads into the much more relaxed notion that while moderation was the ideal it depended on individual will, with whatever minor restrictions and taxes there might be. By the 1860s things were going further, with total bans on alcohol in some places such as parks bequeathed for the public good and the estates of any wealthy landowner committed to the cause. As always, campaigners for reasonable behaviour were slowly forced out of the public eye by those who made louder noises.

Individual MPs made several attempts to introduce 'local option', up to the first decade of the twentieth century when the last to try was Lief Jones (known by some as *tea leaf Jones*), a Hayler associate. Nevertheless, both Scotland and Wales were successful in obtaining Acts. The first-ever piece of Welsh-only legislation, the Sunday Closing (Wales) Act 1881, shut pubs on Sundays and remained partly in force until 1996. The Temperance (Scotland) Act of 1913 allowed local areas to vote on whether to allow alcohol to be sold; after amendment it was in force until 1976. England remained largely untouched until very restrictive provisions on opening hours arrived in the First World War, not significantly relaxed for many decades.

Hayler was among the prominent campaigners for total abstention. He campaigned against what he saw as the worst sins of his day: alcohol and war. The absence of major wars involving the UK before 1914 meant that his interest – one might say obsession – with alcohol was at minimal risk of distraction.

The choice of Guy's Christian name, with its resonance of revolutionary activity, is consistent with his father's support for Chartism. Significantly, the family was dissenting, being Congregationalist. Cresy's report of 1850* suggests that they were at what is now the Pilgrim's Rest.

The family soon moved to Hastings. According to a family report Guy left Sussex at the age of 14, in about 1865. He had converted to the cause of temperance at the very early age of six, presumably

---

* See Chapter 8.

with the support of and perhaps on the insistence of his parents, at a blacksmith's shop in Hastings. By the late 1860s he had gone to London, where he found work as a painter and decorator.

The family account continues:

> Somebody handed him a handbill advertising a meeting to be held in the Exeter Hall, 26 King William Street. This proved to be a great temperance rally and my grandfather became immersed in the cause. He was given the role of steward and attended all the public meetings. In 1870 when he was twenty, he joined another branch of the movement called the Good Templars, an organisation that had Lodges in different parts of the country. This particular lodge was over William Tweedie's bookshop in the Strand.

Exeter Hall, which was to be demolished in 1907, was a great centre for radical causes, among them the abolition of slavery. From 1831 it was also a centre of temperance activity.

Hayler married in 1874. After the marriage he was appointed secretary of the Hull branch of the United Kingdom Alliance, the leading temperance organisation, and he and his wife moved there. Hull was a prosperous shipping port and therefore a good place for any young man to launch a career. They would have eight children: one in London, six in Hull and one in Newcastle on Tyne.

In Hull they ran Haylers Temperance Hotel. On its advertising card there are engravings of the coffee rooms, billiard room, smoke room, commercial room, club room and reading room. It looks quite an impressive place. Guy was also busy at this time organising public meetings and getting involved in all aspects of the temperance movement. In 1889 he rose to a bigger job at Newcastle on Tyne.

There he became full-time secretary of the North of England Temperance League. He worked very hard organising hundreds of rallies, demonstrations and public meetings. One of the most successful events was a grand bazaar opened by Queen Victoria's daughter, Princess Louise. He was now becoming well known as a powerful orator.

Although prohibition was overwhelmingly a working-class movement it had its upper-class adherents. Lady Henry Somerset was one such (she was also a promoter of women's rights). Hayler caught the eye of another upper-class woman, Rosalind Howard, Countess of Carlisle, the châtelaine of Castle Howard in Yorkshire.* She joined the anti-alcohol movement in 1881 and when she had the authority to do so imposed a condition of abstinence on her workers. She much admired Hayler and when he was suffering from overwork in Newcastle she offered him a home and work on her estate. This didn't last long because he inherited a substantial sum from an uncle and moved to Surrey.

Guy Hayler
www.lodgetemperance.org.uk/history/founding-members/bro-guy-hayler

Hayler never wavered in his commitment to the cause and remained active in it until his death. Some British prohibitionists were given

---

* When her husband succeeded to the earldom of Carlisle in 1889 he shut the Castle Howard Brewhouse and all the pubs and beerhouses on his Yorkshire and Cumberland estates.

to admiring, a trifle wistfully, the way the Nazis were apparently tackling the drink problem in Germany. In his presidential address to the 1937 meeting of the World Prohibition Federation in Warsaw, Guy Hayler said the fight against inebriating poisons had enjoyed official patronage and leadership since the advent of Hitler in 1933. Hitler's defects seem to have been overlooked.

Hayler's international involvements were considerable. He went to the USA on various occasions to help and to learn from prohibitionists there, and in 1909 he became the founding honorary president of what became the World Prohibition Federation. He edited its *International Record* until his death. He was a prolific writer of reports and pamphlets, and even has a novel to his name (needless to say, on the subject of teetotalism).

That he was not a single-issue man is shown from his letter to Asquith, the prime minister at the end of 1915. Conscription seemed imminent.

> Dear Sir,
> If it is true that the Government has decided in favour of Conscription, the unity of the nation is gone, and evil times are in store for thousands in this land. For one, and I know there are many more, I shall fight this evil thing for all I am worth. It may mean withdrawing from all the work in which we have been engaged in since this deplorable war began, but in fighting militarism in Germany we never looked for it being planted in our own country. From those I have already seen, who are opposed to conscription, there must be thousands who will not willingly allow it to become law. If you force it through Parliament you will want an army to enforce it. As an old radical I emplore [*sic*] you not to permit this wrong being done. Yours very truly, Guy Hayler.

The family continued in the same strain. Guy's son Glen was called up in the next year and court-martialled for disobeying orders. In defence he stated that he had a long-standing objection to war, that all men were brothers and that differences between them should be settled by peaceful means. He would never go to war and claimed exemption from service on conscientious grounds. Nevertheless he was sentenced to six months' detention.

A similar fate befell his brother Mark, imprisoned on various occasions for his resistance to conscription. He became executive secretary of the World Prohibition Federation in 1925, and editor of the Federation's journal after Guy died. (It ceased publication in 1968.)

As we know, Guy did not achieve his objective, even partially. If drunkenness was a curse in the past, it still is. It remains closely associated with poverty, domestic and street violence and, together with alcoholism, creates serious pressure on an already-overstretched health service. Guy's crusade was far from ignoble, even if when it succeeded in the United States it led to much worse, rather than to better, conditions.

10

Men and Women of War

The UK is no stranger to war. Each century is marked by continual bouts of warfare. Since England and Scotland united in 1707 Britain has been involved in no fewer than 24 major wars, let alone the minor (mostly colonial) ones. The eternal enemy until 1815 was France, but Spain followed it pretty closely.

Some people think that there has been peace since 1945. Such an approach overlooks Korea, Suez and the Falklands as well as continuing involvement in what were colonies or other places where the army or other branches were actively deployed, for example Palestine, Egypt, India, Malaya, Kenya, Sierra Leone, Oman, Kuwait and Iraq, Afghanistan and the former Yugoslavia, and at home in Northern Ireland.

A future General at Québec

James Murray
(1721–1794)

Going back a little, history doesn't record the names of those locals who served in the forces, but for the eighteenth century we know of James Murray of Beauport Park, a distinguished soldier and colonial governor.

Drawn and Engraved expressly for Tuttle's History of the Dominion of Canada.
BATTLE OF THE PLAINS OF ABRAHAM, SEPTEMBER 13th, 1759.

Battle of Quebec

Murray was a younger son of a peer who suffered badly in the financial disaster of 1720 known as the South Sea Bubble. As with so many younger sons of peers, however wealthy or broke, he joined the services; he was 15. The 3rd Scots Regiment was then keeping the peace in what is now Belgium, and he was stationed at Ypres. By 1740 he was a Second Lieutenant in the Marines in the war with

Spain (the War of the Austrian Succession) in the West Indies/South America theatre. In 1744 he was part of a unit sent to Hastings to help the struggle against smugglers (and there he met his future wife). After various tours he found himself in the Seven Years War and was sent to Canada in 1758 as part of the force ordered to take the colony of Québec from the French.

Famously victory was won and in 1763, when peace returned, he was appointed Military Governor of Québec, where he made every effort to avoid alienating the French colonists there. In 1764 he summed up his own views:

> Little, very little, will content the new subjects [the French Canadians] but nothing will satisfy the licentious fanatics trading here but the expulsion of the Canadians who are perhaps the bravest and the best race upon the globe, a race who, could they be indulged with a few privileges which the laws of England deny to Roman Catholics at home, would soon get the better of every national antipathy to their conquerors and become the most faithful and most useful set of men in the American empire...

THE HON. LIEUT.-GENERAL JAMES MURRAY.
From a print of about the year 1773.
By kind permission of the Clarendon Press, Oxford.

From Tuttle's *History of the Dominion of Canada*

His successor took the same line, against instructions.

Removed from office there, he became Lieutenant Governor of the British colony of Minorca in 1774 and Governor five years later (where an earlier governor, Richard Kane, had kept the peace in the same way as Murray did in Québec); but the island was overwhelmed by the Spanish and French in 1781 and had to surrender. Perhaps because of memories of the unfortunate Admiral Byng (executed in 1757 for his failure to relieve Minorca), a disgruntled former colleague made accusations of dereliction of duty against him. Murray asked for a court martial against himself, at which he was acquitted. He was promoted General in 1783.

It was at Hastings that Murray came across the Collier family. It's hard to overestimate the influence of John Collier, one of whose daughters Murray married, or of his growing wealth. Originally from Eastbourne, he was appointed town clerk of Hastings and established close relationships with powerful people of the area, including (at a predictable distance) the Dukes of Newcastle, successive prime ministers and major Sussex landowners based at Laughton near Lewes. It's also hard now to believe the extent of corruption that characterised British politics: it certainly characterised Hastings. Collier and his relations the Milwards dominated the town and kept it politically safe for Newcastle.

This extended family included the Denhams, who had bought Beacon Hill on what was to become Beauport estate and were building a large house there, and the Worges who were to buy a large part of the Battle Abbey estate.

This set may or may not have had deals with the smugglers through Collier running the local customs service, but bribes elsewhere would have been common. Somehow the Hastings Book of Records was lost (probably deliberately), which was effectively the constitution of the town. Collier built up a large estate in and around Hastings and amassed a fortune.

Murray was not party to the corruption but he benefited from it. Because of his career, he was not at Hastings for long periods, though for some years he was a jurat (a kind of mixture of alderman and magistrate) until the Milwards had him deposed. In 1748 he married Cordelia Collier and without the help of her dowry bought himself the rank of Major. By the time he returned from his governorship of Québec Collier had died, having adjusted his will to assign the dowry to him. Murray now had lots of money.

In 1762 he bought the Denham estate, which included parts of the town. The main part was in the parish of Battle. There he had a fine house built, probably incorporating part of Beacon Hill, but he couldn't escape further military service until 1783.

Then he retired to the new house, named Beauport Park after the place from which the assault on Québec had been launched. His son did not wish to take it and soon it went to the Burges family, which had the distinction of having captured the standard of the Young Pretender at the battle of Culloden in 1746; Burges was a baronet and as a condition of the purchase he was obliged to change his name to Lamb, a major personal benefactor. It remained with that family until sold in 1922.

Architect's design for Beauport House in Murray's time, found in Murray's papers

In 1923 the house was very seriously damaged by fire and rebuilt. A grandson of 'Violet Fane' bought it and turned it into a hotel; it now performs a number of functions as a health spa. It keeps the same appearance of the middle part as Murray had, but much was destroyed and the two wings are modern.

He ended Wellington's revelry by night

❦

Sir Henry Webster
(1793–1847)

For the revolutionary and Napoleonic wars of 1793–1815 the best-known Battle man was of the Webster family of Battle Abbey:

Webster was responsible for an event made memorable by Lord Byron. The first two stanzas of the nine constituting *The Eve of Waterloo are:*

> There was a sound of revelry by night,
>   And Belgium's Capital had gathered then
>   Her Beauty and her Chivalry, and bright
>   The lamps shone o'er fair women and brave men;
>   A thousand hearts beat happily; and when
>   Music arose with its voluptuous swell,
>   Soft eyes looked love to eyes which spake again,
>   And all went merry as a marriage bell,
> But hush! Hark! A deep sound strikes like a rising knell!
>
> Did ye not hear it? – No; 'twas but the wind,
>   Or the car rattling o'er the stony street;
>   On with the dance! Let joy be unconfined;
>   No sleep till morn, when Youth and Pleasure meet
>   To chase the glowing Hours with flying feet –
>   But hark! – that heavy sound breaks in once more,
>   As if the clouds its echo would repeat;
>   And nearer, clearer, deadlier than before!
> Arm! Arm! It is – it is – the cannon's opening roar!

Whether cannon could be heard at Brussels is doubtful, particularly after nightfall when battles ceased, even with a full moon. But we do know that a Battle man brought to the ball the news of the French arrival at Quatre Bras, resulting in the rapid deployment of all Wellington's soldiers to the battle threatened there. This was in the night of 15-16 June and not, as one might infer from the poem's title, 17 June. The man bringing the news was Henry Vassall Webster, brother of the then baronet.

One writer states that Webster had been invited to the ball but was unable to attend:

> Between 11pm & midnight, Wellington went to the Duchess of Richmond's Ball; he could not have been there long when (about 1 a m) Lt Henry Webster of the 9th Light Dragoons attached to the Prince of Orange's staff, arrived.
>
> Breathless and covered in dust and foam, he was carrying urgent news. The message Webster was carrying had left Braine-le-Comte at 10.30pm covering the distance to Brussels at high speed.* He had ridden first to Wellington's HQ in the Rue Royale in Brussels.
>
> Finding that the Duke of Wellington and the Prince of Orange had already left for the Ball, a servant led him to its venue. They reached there after midnight. Here Webster handed the despatch to the Prince of Orange. The letter, from (Maj Gen Jean-Victor) Constant Rebecque contained the news that the French, who had crossed the Sambre river, invading Belgium early that morning, had that evening broken through to Quatre Bras.
>
> Communications with the Prussian HQ in Sombreffe were therefore threatened. Napoleon was on the point of successfully driving a wedge between the two wings of the Allied forces which he then hoped to defeat in detail. A perplexed Prince of Orange passed the news to a dumbfounded Duke. Now, and only now, did Wellington accept the seriousness of the situation.

The messenger himself wrote later:

I was in my saddle without a second's delay; and, thanks to a fine moon and two capital horses, had covered the ten miles I had to go within the hour! Such was the crowd of carriages, that I could not

---

* Braine-le-Comte is about 24km (about 15 miles) southwest of Brussels.

well make my way through them on horseback; so I abandoned my steed to the first man I could get hold of, and made my way on foot to the porter's lodge.

Wellington brought the ball to an abrupt end by ordering all officers to report to their regiments, though he did allow those on the dance floor to finish their dances. The battle of Quatre Bras on the next day would stop Napoleon's splitting the British and Prussian forces. It allowed the final battle to be won at Waterloo.

Webster was a Lieutenant in the 9th Light Dragoon Guards and ADC to the Prince of Orange. By 1824 he was a Captain, then Lieutenant Colonel and finally a full colonel in 1831; he was knighted in 1843. Along the way he collected various medals, including the Waterloo Medal and three non-British knighthoods: Willem of the Netherlands, and the Tower and Sword and San Bento d'Avis, both of Portugal. He had joined the Light Dragoon Guards as a Cornet in March 1810, being promoted Lieutenant in June 1811, and was slightly wounded at Vitoria in 1813. Webster was tall: 6' 8" by one account.

Like his parents, Webster became involved in a divorce, still a very public matter. In 1824, Henry Baring MP accused him of seducing his wife. Webster did not defend himself and suffered damages of £1,000, though £10,000 had been sought. In October of the same year he married Grace Boddington and they were to have two children.

In 1847 he committed suicide at his Mayfair house by cutting his throat with a penknife. The doctors attending the body attested to his unsound mind, and the coroner's jury agreed a verdict that the deceased died from the effects of wounds inflicted on himself while labouring under temporary insanity. His father had done the same, by shooting himself.

His body was placed in the vault at St Mary's, Battle. His sword is in the possession of Ralfe Whistler of Battle.

The woman on First World War service

❧

Margaret Joan Ashton, later Whistler
(1893–1981)

J oan Ashton, a daughter of Lord Ashton of Hyde, married into the Whistler family of Battle after the First World War. Her father's fortune came from the cotton mills of Hyde in Cheshire, an environment as distant from that of Battle as can be imagined. He was not just an industrialist but was involved in politics, and he was awarded his peerage in 1911. By then he had bought Vine Hall in the parish of Mountfield.

Joan Ashton

Joan served throughout the First World War, starting as a welder with the Royal Naval Air Service (at a time when the supply of effective welders' masks, made in Germany, were no longer available, so leading to cases of optical damage). Then she served with the Army Service Corps, driving empty lorry chassis to coachbuilders in England and then much more dangerously transporting shell supplies from the Rouen area to the front in France. These transports would not have had power-assisted steering and the roads would not have been good; she must have been pretty tough physically. Her service is peculiar in that she appears to have been a regular member of the ASC (MT/) at a time when women had their own services.

Like other members of the Watts and Whistler families she is commemorated in a corner of St Mary's church at Battle.

The army chaplain who overpowered his captor

❧❦

Alfred Thomas Arthur Naylor
(1889–1966)

N aylor was Dean of Battle from 1946 to 1960. He had had a distinguished military career as an army chaplain.

Cap badge for the Royal Army Chaplains' Department, First World War

He had been born at Hucknall in Nottinghamshire, son of a Congregational minister rather than of an Anglican. Ordained as a priest in 1913, not long after leaving Cambridge, he became curate at Pudsey in the West Riding. The First World War began very shortly and he volunteered to become an army chaplain. He was gassed and wounded at Ypres in 1915 but returned to the forces, being Mentioned in Despatches. At the end of the war he was awarded the OBE (Military). He remained an army chaplain throughout the inter-war period, which included postings to China and Palestine.

In 1940 he again went abroad with the army. He was taken by the Germans during the retreat to Dunkirk but with the help of his driver he overpowered their captor and after swimming a canal they managed to be evacuated. He was again Mentioned in Despatches and shortly after his escape he was awarded the DSO. He was appointed an Honorary Chaplain to the King in 1945 and a Deputy Chaplain General. On his retirement he lived at Home Place, Whatlington.

The youngest female soldier
to die in service

✑✦✦✑

Violet Edith Akehurst
(1925–1941)

The sixteen-year old Violet never had a chance to become a heroine. However, she is remembered today as being the youngest British or Commonwealth woman to die in military service in the Second World War.

Violet Akehurst (service picture inset)
photo by Peter Greene from two originals

In some ways this was already an unfortunate family. Violet's father Alec, who was recorded in 1939 as a gypsum miner, above ground but nevertheless engaged in what was termed heavy work, married Edith MacDonald in 1918. They had eight children, three of whom died in infancy. The survivors moved to Battle in about 1928 and by 1939 they were at the newly-built 4 Coronation Gardens. Violet's first newspaper appearance was in September 1941 when she was a bridesmaid at the marriage of her sister Florence; the second and last was her In memoriam notice in 1942.

Her war service was brief. After her sixteenth birthday in August 1941 she joined up as a Private in the Auxiliary Territorial Service and was posted to the 490th Heavy Anti-Aircraft Battery of the Royal Artillery. This was deployed at Richmond Park in Surrey and was the first base to have members of both sexes there. It seems likely that Violet was there.

Young people were, and still are, prone to meningitis, and she contracted the pneumococcal strain. There was effectively no treatment available, and even if it had been it would have to have been applied very early. She was taken to Bath military hospital and died there on 25 November. Her grave is marked by a military headstone in a lonely part of Battle cemetery.

None of her family appears now to live in Sussex.

The airman who escaped from a POW camp

John Shore
(1917–1950)

Shore is notable less for his war service than for being one of those who made successful escapes from German prisoner-of-war camps. He had come to Battle at the age of four and as a very young man he worked at Vicary's Garage; he married his first wife at St Mary's in 1939.

Shore joined the RAF when he was 19, in 1936, and after training joined Bomber Command. Bombing an enemy target was a most dangerous matter, and about 60% of British crews did not survive. The navigators had to find the target, and the bombs were meant to fall in the right place, which was very often not the case. All the time the crews were themselves targets of anti-aircraft shells on land and bullets from airborne fighters. Shore's own report suggests that the target on 27 March 1941 was Cologne. Searches of relevant records throw doubt on its precision but it was almost certainly in that area that his aircraft was, he thought, damaged; on the return flight both engines failed over the Netherlands. The crew left by parachute.

Shore received much help from sympathetic local people, but he had to be handed over to the Germans. He was then taken across most of Germany to Stalag Luft 1 at Barth, northwest of Stralsund and close to the Baltic coast; he tried to escape from a train taking him there. He and others planned to leave the camp by tunnel, though none of them had identity papers of any sort and Shore did not speak German. He managed to get through the tunnel and then had to walk some 40 miles (65 km) to the port of Sassnitz and smuggle himself on a ferry to Trelleborg in Sweden. He managed this partly by the failure of local German guards to do their duty. From Sweden he was flown back to the UK where he became a test pilot for aircraft then being developed.

After the war he left the RAF. He later rejoined, but was killed when his craft crashed into Snowdon.

An SOE man in
France and Burma

❦

Thomas Arthur Carew
(1920–2009)

C arew was one of those remarkable people who went behind
the lines during the Second World War, killing the enemy
where they could and damaging their communication lines,
helping local people resist the invaders and providing London with
accurate information. They put their lives at serious risk, for capture
meant certain death. Carew ended with the DSO and the French
Croix de Guerre. He spent some of his old age at Battle.

Carew had been born in Dublin but his family soon left Ireland,
for there was considerable disorder and anti-British feeling. He was
commissioned in 1939 and served in Norway and Gibraltar. He
must have come to the notice of his seniors because later he joined
the Special Operations Executive (SOE). This was a highly-secret
force initiated by Winston Churchill and established by Neville
Chamberlain, his immediate predecessor as Prime Minister. It was
to 'co-ordinate all action, by way of subversion and sabotage, against
the enemy overseas'.

There were few rules about recruitment other than calmness,
fitness, intelligence, resourcefulness and training, and a significant
proportion of the agents were women. Among those who supported
their training were former criminals who were expert, for example, in
forging banknotes; others told them how to carry out silent killing.

Carew's first SOE mission was to German-occupied France on
26 August 1944. He must have known what capture would have
meant, and each agent was given a cyanide pill to take in such a case.
(They also had a supply of forged banknotes to encourage further

co-operation by the French.) The Germans had already been beaten back from the Normandy beaches and on 15 August the Allies had landed on the Mediterranean coast.

The Germans would do almost anything to keep possession of France. In turn SOE would do almost anything to stop them sending reinforcements to either front line. Among other things this meant destroying railway lines and creating so much trouble that many Germans were kept behind to control the areas concerned.

It must have been hard for them to secure rural France, and the area south of Besançon near the Swiss border was well-wooded and hilly. This was perfect territory for ambushing Germans, and a good few were killed there. Carew's force was part of a larger group that captured small towns and took Germans captive.

Returning to Britain later in the year he prepared for an even bigger task: Burma, where the Japanese occupiers were more cruel to those captured even than the Germans were and where the risk of serious disease was much greater. He landed in the Arakan area late in 1944. It may have been the opium that he carried for in no time he had recruited and organised a small army of 400 local hillmen. He was an independent leader, left to do his best, which he did: killing Japanese and capturing or destroying their weapons and supplies. His resourcefulness is shown by occasions on which to mislead the enemy he and his men went backwards, their footsteps telling the Japanese that they had gone to the place that they had actually just left.

There was a practical problem not faced in France: the Burmese had already formed an army aimed at pushing the British out of their country. This army now realised that the Japanese were even less likely to grant independence and were a much nastier occupying force than the British. When they came over to the Allied side the British authorities started to arrest their leaders for treason but Carew intervened and managed to save them, and by extension their adherence to ousting the Japanese.

Thereafter his London superiors stopped having anything to do with the civilian authorities, which helped a great deal. The British 14th Army worked closely with the Burmese army, to which Carew was attached, and the alliance was of enormous assistance.

It continued to be threatened by the colonial administration but the Supreme Commander, Lord Louis Mountbatten, managed to preserve it, if only with difficulty.

SOE was disbanded early in 1946 and Carew returned to the army with the DSO. He had several overseas postings before leaving it in 1958. Thereafter there were several jobs before retiring to Battle, living at 20 Upper Lake. All his three wives predeceased him.

Killed by the Irgun in Palestine

❧❧

Geoffrey Hildebrand
(1905–1948)

The blue gates to St Catherine's Chapel in St Mary's church at Battle commemorate Lt Col Geoffrey Hildebrand DSO, who died in Palestine very close to the end of British involvement there, on 6 April 1948. The 12th Anti-Tank Regiment of the Royal Artillery were involved in evacuating a large camp near Pardes Hanna a little south of Haifa when they were attacked by men from the Zionist Irgun organisation. The sentry and three other members of the guard were held against the guardhouse wall, shot in the back, and killed. The wireless mast was then destroyed, and shots fired into the camp, killing three more soldiers and mortally injuring Hildebrand. By any reckoning this was terrorism and needlessly so, because the British had already started to leave the country and were only some five weeks away from their final departure.

It might not be clear why he is commemorated at Battle. Geoffrey Lancelot Hildebrand was from Kent, but his home was at Mill Farm, Higham, in Suffolk. His father Arthur had served in the army and had risen to be a Brigadier General in the Royal Engineers. He was unmarried.

The gates were erected when the Dean was Alfred Naylor. Given his own record above he must have been sympathetic to commemorating a military death.

The decision to proceed with the gates and the memorial plaque was taken at the prompting of a doctor at Battle, Tom Nevill-Wood. He had married Hildebrand's sister and was an executor of Hildebrand's will. He was about to retire from his practice. They paid for the gates.

Memorial plaque to Geoffrey Hildebrand on gates in St Mary's Church, photo by Peter Greene

11
Landlords' tales

E very rural area used to be subject to its landowners. They were men (and sometimes women) rarely of particular distinction other than in their inheritance but they were magistrates, high sheriffs, MPs and so on because hardly anyone else would have had their education and because it had always been so.

They have almost all gone now. Only one such landlord family survives in a large house in the Battle area occupied by the family since the middle of the nineteenth century, and they don't exercise the traditional functions. But up to 1914 all landlords were certainly the bosses.

This chapter includes some landlords of Battle Abbey, the famous 'Mad Jack' Fuller of Brightling, Moreton Frewen of Brede Place and the Brassey family; the artist Hercules Brabazon Brabazon, owner of Oaklands, is considered in Chapter 3. There is also the controversial Alfred Milner who was heavily involved in South African affairs and provoked the war of 1899–1902. Some appear elsewhere in this book.

The curse on the Abbey's families

◈◈◈

Brownes, Websters, Clevelands, Websters again and after

In 1538 the dissolved monasteries were now part of the king's estate and he could pass them on to his favourites as he wished. The lucky man for Battle was Sir Anthony Browne. He was a loyal servant of Henry VIII in various capacities including Master of the Horse and ambassador to France.

The now-dissolved abbey was hardly in a condition fit for a major landlord of the time, for he would be expected to entertain in grand style. He first had the now superfluous abbey church knocked down, and perhaps it was this single act that provoked the legendary (or mythical) curse.

The story goes that when Browne was entertaining guests, a monk pushed his way into the Abbey and shouted his curse, to the effect that its owners would die by fire or water. Whether fantasy or the truth it was believed by people in the Battle area later, certainly by the nineteenth century, and with good reason.

Browne himself died in 1548, presumably not in the accursed manner, and he is now remembered by the remarkable alabaster tomb of him and his first wife Alys close to the altar at St Mary's church just across the road from the abbey.

His son succeeded and became Viscount Montagu, a peerage named after a grandfather's marquessate. It was probably he who built a two-story block close to the abbey (demolished in the eighteenth century) of which only two towers and the cellars remain. The Brownes stayed Catholic for a long time, being awarded the viscountcy by Queen Mary and being involved in her pursuit of 'heretics'. But they remained in royal favour throughout the reign of Elizabeth. Montagu's wife outlived him into the reign of James I, being the centre of a local Catholic group.*

It may be that Battle became less comfortable for the Brownes than it had been, and the family moved to the larger, Tudor, Cowdray House near Midhurst, taking with them many documents and artefacts and presumably leaving the Abbey empty. If the curse went with them it took quite a while to act. In September 1793 Cowdray House was destroyed by fire. (Unfortunately many things removed from the Abbey were destroyed by it.) The eighth viscount was on holiday elsewhere in Europe and a few days after the fire he chose to take a boat down some rapids on the upper Rhine. The boat overturned and the viscount drowned. Four years later his uncle died and the title became extinct.

The curse had worked.

By 1793 the Abbey had long been in the possession of the baronets of the Webster family. They had bought it in 1721 and for a while they ran it well, even extending the estate. But towards the end of the century things began to go wrong.

The fourth baronet, often thought not to be entirely sane by his fellow-MPs, is a story in Chapters 1 and 2. He had been an inveterate gambler and womaniser. His successor, also Godfrey, was at least financially no better (in the 1820s the Abbey was leased out), and when he died in 1836 his estate was in a poor financial condition. Large parts were sold off but that proved no answer. By 1857 there was no alternative but to sell it all. It went to the extraordinarily wealthy Lord Harry Vane, later the fourth and last Duke of Cleveland. When he died his widow continued to live there until her death in 1901.

As fourth duke he looks as if he came from a long line with that title. Actually his father had received the honour only in 1833, and none of his three sons had any heirs. The Battle inheritor was the youngest and last. But there is no hint anywhere that his death, or that of his widow, was caused by the curse.

This family was immensely wealthy, and the Duke left the sum of just over £1,449,000 – in today's money the lowest equivalent is some

---

* See Chapter 5.

£159 million and the highest over two thousand million. The family had long owned land and had profited from the growth of mining in their home area, the north-east of England. The Duke was a KG and a prominent Whig politician who was once seriously considered for the post of prime minister. He married a widow, the mother of the man who was to become the fifth Earl of Rosebery and actually was prime minister in 1894–95 (his odd but memorable distinction being that in both years of his prime ministership his horse won the Derby).

Having lost her second husband, the Duchess continued living at the Abbey until her death in Germany. This meant that the Websters could return, and perhaps the curse might then perform its duty. The family bought back the estate in 1902.

The then baronet, Sir Augustus, had married a woman whose considerable wealth was founded on the work of a carpet manufacturer, but they still had to sell quite large parts of the estate. They chose to live in the more comfortable house at Powdermill, leasing the abbey to Michael Grace, an Irish-American businessman. They sold the more expensive contents, netting more than £17,000.

In the summer of 1917 things went badly wrong. In June Lady Webster was watching one of her daughters swimming in Farthing Pond near Battle and saw her get into difficulties. She and a maid jumped in. The maid brought the daughter to the edge of the water, but Lady Webster drowned. Six weeks later her only son and the last heir to the baronetcy was in the third Battle of Ypres. A shell fell at his feet, killing him instantly. In this case water and fire. (Only some two weeks later the eldest daughter of Michael Grace, who had only just left the Abbey, was drowned in Italy.)

Sir Augustus cannot be blamed for a deep sorrow that may have led to rather too much fondness for bottled goods; he presumably had thought that he was founding a refreshed dynasty to continue for many years, and this disappointment must have struck him deeply quite apart from the double shock that caused him such personal loss.

He seemed to be much less co-operative with the town after the war. He struggled hard to avoid selling the land that became Wellington Gardens, leading to a remark by a councillor: "I thought that spirit was dead and gone. Is that what England has been saved for?" There was also a continuing argument about the use of what is now the Abbey Green. Deference was almost over.

Sir Augustus died in 1923 at the age of only 59. His heiress Lucy reported that he had General Paralysis of the Insane, the final stage of syphilis; the local newspaper referred to strokes. The funeral was attended by a very large number of local people. Some of the estate was then sold, the rest in 1976.

Augustus left two daughters. The estate was in the hands of trustees, though technically it belonged to the elder daughter Lucy.

Her sister Evelyn was unhappy in a different way from Lucy. She married and had two sons but parted from their father and resumed her maiden name. She was one of those who greeted the Queen when she came to Battle for the 900th anniversary of the Battle of Hastings. Evelyn seems to have had a strong feeling that she was the *grande dame* of the area. She strongly opposed the sale of the Abbey and the remaining estate in 1976, but the trustees had the last word.

Before her death in 1988 her elder son Godfrey Harbord took to calling himself Sir Godfrey Webster but it was a false claim: a baronetcy can descend only to and through males. His death in 2003 did not quite end the recent Webster line: his brother Simon, who died before him, had had a son who has a family of his own.

After Michael Grace's tenancy the Abbey tenant for a few months was the Belgian, Paul Waterkeyn. In 1922 it was leased to what was to be called Battle Abbey School – and still is. The serious fire there in 1931 was extinguished by water (but there were no deaths).

'Mad Jack' Fuller

❧

John Fuller
(1757–1834)

A favourite hobby of authors is to write accounts of English eccentrics. Their books are many and they can be very entertaining. It's rarely that they don't include 'Mad Jack' Fuller of Brightling Park. Clearly Jack wasn't mad – at least not compared with his contemporary John Mytton of Shropshire (whose extraordinary behaviour isn't to be explored here). Nor was he eccentric. He was just so independent of mind that he tended to veer from the conventional picture of the wealthy landowner.

Locally Jack is now known mainly for his extensions to Brightling Park, which he and his father called Rose Hill after his grandmother's family name, and nationally for his benevolence to scientific researchers, but the 'eccentrics' authors can find out much more. A story goes that in London he laid a bet that he could see Dallington church from his house but on his return home he found that he couldn't, so he built the forty-foot Sugar Loaf Folly in the right direction to give the impression that he was right. One hopes that he told his friend the truth.

As to his future death he declined to be buried. Along the lines of the traditional song *On Ilkley Moor baht 'at* he took the view that worms would eat him; ducks would eat the worms; his family would eat the ducks. And he had no wish to be eaten by his family, or indeed by anyone else. So in 1810 he built a pyramidal mausoleum in Brightling churchyard in which his body was to be placed, seated at a table with a bottle of claret. To await the arrival of the devil to claim him he ordered broken glass to be scattered around the floor so that Satan might at least cut his feet. We know from a later opening of the pyramid that he was buried conventionally, or so those responsible

The Brightling mausoleum,
origin of photograph unknown

reported. We know anyway that he was a bit of a joker.

Unlike Mytton in some his exploits, he harmed no-one, at least in this country: his acts were minor and often charming. But he was different. It is said that he declined Pitt's offer of a peerage with the words, "I was born Jack Fuller and Jack Fuller I will die". Pitt probably just wanted him out of the Commons, where he was something of a nuisance.

The family's wealth was built on the Wealden iron industry and the estate had come to them in 1697. They made many improvements and extensions to the estate and the house. John Fuller (1680–1745) married Elizabeth Rose, a Jamaican heiress who brought a considerable fortune to the family along with extensive estates in the West Indies of over 1215ha (about 3,000 acres).

He rebuilt the house on a grander scale and enlarged the estate to 526ha (1,300 acres). He laid out a deer park around the house, the park being bounded on its east, south and west sides by a tributary of the Darwell stream. He diverted a road leading past the north front of the house and acquired a long lease of land on Brightling Hill, as sheep grazing. He started planting the park with clumps of trees and built a Chinese temple and a keep in the grounds.

Particularly in the naturalistic use of water his work on the estate included five ponds and anticipated the style of Capability Brown, then not begun on his notable career. He left the estate to his second son Rose (yes, a son). Rose had managed the Jamaican estates, winning a fierce reputation for discipline before being dismissed as Chief Justice of the colony.

Jack was the next in line, son of Rose's brother Henry, who had already died. Henry had been vicar of North Stoneham near Southampton, where Jack had been born.

When Jack came of age he had all the opportunities of a rich and landed gentleman. He was elected MP for Southampton at the age of 22, a seat he held for four years; his uncle by marriage, Hans Sloane (also a major slave-owner and great-nephew of the better known Hans Sloane), was the other member.

He was an engaging young man:

> Captain Fuller ... has an estate of £4000 or £5000 a year, is but just of age, has figure, understanding, education, vivacity, and independence, and yet voluntarily devotes almost all his time, and almost all his attention to a company of light infantry.

Mrs Thrale, a brewery heiress and one-time friend of Samuel Johnson, had described him in *Thraliana* (29 January 1781) as 'wild, gay, rich, loud'; and wrote in a letter to Fanny Burney, 7 February 1781:

> Captain Fuller flashes away among us. How that boy loves rough merriment! the people all seem to keep out of his way for fear.

Jack proposed marriage to Mrs Thrale's daughter but she refused him. In the end he married no-one. Nor are there any known children.

In 1801 he was elected MP for Sussex, and from then he began to attract more serious notice. He spoke frequently, and by today's standards he was notably reactionary if in some limited ways less selfish than some other members. He vigorously opposed softening the penal code and any of the rules against Roman Catholics; he had no time for the Irish.

He must have disliked many fellow-members, whom he believed

were there for their own benefit and not for that of the country, so he supported the abolition of the many sinecures often given to MPs that paid well but involved no duties. Most of all he looked after his own interests: protecting the sugar trade and vigorously opposing the abolition of the slave trade. He opposed the founding of the Sierra Leone colony intended to contain freed slaves brought over from North America. One is tempted to wonder whether the memorials to him at Brightling will be allowed to survive.

He was a blunt speaker and apt to give offence. In 1810 he went so far as to use seriously unparliamentary language – for example calling the Speaker *'the insignificant little fellow in a wig'* and was ordered to withdraw; he refused and was removed by force. But he apologised and was soon back in the chamber. He retired in 1812.

If the above sounds unpleasant to the modern ear, he had a positive and beneficial side. He strongly supported the Royal Institution in London, founded in 1799. In 1828, having already given it substantial funds, he established the Fuller Medal there and in 1833 founded the Fullerian Professorship of Chemistry, the first appointment to which was Michael Faraday. He also founded the Fullerian Professorship of Physiology. Both appointments continue today. In 1834 it was estimated that his support for the Institution by then had reached some £10,000, a very large sum for the day.

Jack redesigned the estate. There is book of plans by Humphrey Repton from 1806–07, but very little of his advice was taken. Brightling Park house is listed Grade II. The architect Robert Smirke, whose works adorn inner London – the frontage of the British Museum is his, among other works – extended it in 1810–12 but unfortunately this part was demolished in 1955. The eighteenth-century stables (Grade II) survive.

'Mad Jack' was a man of considerable energy and enthusiasm, befriending the artist Turner, who made four watercolours of the area. Smirke built the temple, the needle (obelisk), the sugar loaf and the observatory, the last in 1818. (It was a working observatory, by no means a folly: it had an up-to-date telescope made by Sir William Herschel, the discoverer of Uranus.) These buildings are all listed Grade II*.

As well as building on his estate and surrounding most of it with

JACK FULLER.
A DEPARTED FRIEND TO SCIENCE.

London. Published by J.W. Fores at Picadilly, 1833.

a wall (costing some £10,000), Jack funded the building of the Belle Tout lighthouse on Beachy Head, now succeeded by that on the shore below, as well as the first of Sussex's lifeboats, at Eastbourne.

In 1828 he bought Bodiam Castle for the very large sum of £3,300 and saved it from destruction, though its full safeguarding was not assured until nearly a century later. Emergency work kept it standing in the mid-century but its future had to wait on the extraordinary Lord Curzon.

Curzon was one of the best-known politicians of the thirty years before his death. Born into a wealthy noble family, after Eton he went to Balliol College, Oxford. There his self-assurance bordering on arrogance was clear to all. A ditty about him appeared while he was there:

> My name is George Nathaniel Curzon,
> I am a most superior person.

My cheek is pink, my hair is sleek,
I dine at Blenheim once a week

Curzon as Viceroy of India

In 1885 he was elected as an MP and took junior government offices in 1891–92 and 1895–98, then being appointed Viceroy of India (1899–1905). While there he was instrumental in restoring the Taj Mahal at Agra and on his return bought and restored Tattershall Castle in Lincolnshire. In 1916 he was appointed to the Cabinet as part of the coalition government, and was Foreign Secretary from 1919 to 1924. He gave his name to the Curzon Line, the proposed eastern border of the newly-recreated state of Poland, which was to come into effect rather later, with some adjustments, in 1945.

He bought Bodiam Castle in 1917. With minor later repairs, what one sees today is mostly the final restoration carried out under Curzon's instructions. His will bequeathed both Bodiam and Tattershall to the National Trust.

Back to Fuller. He was a benefactor of Brightling church, donating money for improvements and the purchase of an organ; his bust and a plaque are there today.

As Jack had had no children, Rose Hill descended to a cousin, who was a typical country gentleman and MP for Eastern Sussex from 1841 until just before his death in 1857; he had the good fortune to receive Jack's substantial compensation payment for the abandonment of slavery under the 1833 Act. This came to £3895 7s 6d for the Knollis plantation and £762 16s 10d for Grange Pen – the lowest 2019 estimate of its value in 2019 was about £417,000 but the possibilities above that are very high. 253 slaves were freed.

'Mortal Ruin' at Brede Place

Moreton Frewen
(1853–1924)

Brede Place is a house with ancient origins. For a long time it belonged to the Oxenbridge family, and to most people the only interesting Oxenbridge would be Sir Goddard, who was a courtier to Henry VIII and died in 1531: he was reputed to eat naughty children. Clearly, however, this was bruited about as a means of keeping bothersome kids away from his property. E V Lucas, in his *Highways and Byways of East Sussex* (1937) reports that a story that it was once a smuggling headquarters, with an underground passage leading to the distant church, and that to keep nosy people away the smugglers reported that it was haunted. Well...

A much later Brede owner who broke the conventions of squirearchical life was (Hugh) Moreton Frewen. His story is one of constant over-investment and financial failure, which caused some wit to name him Mortal Ruin – when he died in 1924 he left less than £50 – but of great hospitality and a lasting marriage even though he appears to have been a serial adulterer. Moreton started out well enough in the conventional way (Cambridge and the Inner Temple) but he could never keep still. Ventures in the western USA brought in money for a time but then failed heavily, and the same in Australia; when he was left a house in Ireland with a good income he invested heavily again and lost again. (This house was to be burned down by nationalists more extreme than he was.)

He obtained Brede Place in 1898 by purchase from his Northiam brother Edward, and presumably his wife was the source of the money needed; certainly the deeds of property were put in her name to forestall creditors. She was Clara Jerome, whom he had met in New York, the sister of Jennie who had married Lord Randolph

Brede Place, 1899, by Frederick Griggs
From E V Lucas *op. cit.*

Churchill. So Moreton became an uncle of Winston Churchill. He was soon commissioned by the young Churchill to edit one of his books, which he appears to have done very badly.

The house was barely habitable. The Frewens' daughter Clare reported that Brede Place was in a terrible condition. While some Tudor woodwork was in reasonable condition the floors and windows were rarely in good order. Birds infested it. The only two weather-proof rooms were inhabited by a gamekeeper.

To restore the house to a habitable condition, including the installation of running water and lavatories, took some time, during which the American author Stephen Crane* briefly took the lease before going to Germany to die of tuberculosis. When reasonable conditions had been achieved nothing stopped the Frewens from entertaining their guests.

From this account he sounds very much like a failure. In fact, Frewen was a most intelligent, analytical and positive man, with his own very independent views. He wrote well and copiously. His obituary in *The Times* declared:

---

* See Chapter 2

198

There was no more interesting raconteur, and with Mr [Maynard] Keynes he must be accounted one of those Cambridge economists who write as brilliantly as novelists.

The reference to writing rings few bells now but a number of his books appear on second-hand book websites.

According to Kipling, he lived in every sense except what is called common sense, very richly and wisely to his own extreme content, and if he had ever reached the golden crock of his dreams he would have perished. Stephen Crane had earlier said that Frewen, "seemed like a search-light on a hungry boat at sea."

Frewen knew most of the British literati of his age, including Henry James, Joseph Conrad, J M Barrie, Rudyard Kipling and H G Wells, and, as noted above, Stephen Crane. He also moved in circles near, if not actually close to, the throne. He was at almost every upper-class ceremony, whether wedding, funeral or memorial service. In 1913 he was part of the 'peace delegation' sent to the USA to celebrate the century of peace following the 1812–14 war between the two countries.

His first letter to *The Times* was in 1884, when he was heavily involved with attempts to open the British market to beef imports from the USA; the last was to be not long before he died. They were on a range of subjects – not only beef imports but salmon hatcheries, relations with the USA, the currency of India and the constitution of the UK (for which he championed a federal arrangement of five states – presumably England, Scotland, Wales and two parts of Ireland). In December 1910, to general surprise, he was elected unopposed as MP for North East Cork, standing as an Independent Nationalist.

At that time there were two Irish nationalist parties in the Commons – the majority led by William Redmond, and the independents led by William O'Brien. Redmond wanted a fully united Ireland; the latter favoured concessions to the North, to be included in an Ireland that would give powers to its devolved provinces.

Frewen did not last long in the Commons. As soon as he was elected he was saying that he wanted to resign and make way for Tim Healy (who was later to be Governor-General of the Irish Free State) but the moment did not come until later. An argumentative parliamentarian, he tended to disagree with any party line, and wanted to oppose the Bill then being debated on the future of the House of Lords. Instead of simply limiting its powers, he wanted it replaced altogether by his proposed federal body; but he was almost alone in this view, even among his immediate colleagues. (It is a view that still has some traction, not noticeably among members of either House of Parliament.) He would have been pleased that Healy was indeed elected in his place, unopposed.

Earlier in the century he had been a leading light in the Tariff Reform League in the debates on the future of free trade that led to the Conservative Party splitting and the great Liberal victory in the general election of 1906, by way of writing articles and touring the country making speeches. The Frewens left a notable addition to the artistic scene: their daughter Clare,* who as Clare Sheridan became a well-known sculptress.

Brede was sold in 1936. It has since been seriously damaged by fire but rebuilt.

---

* See Chapter 3

The railway heirs

❦

The Brassey family

T he Brasseys rose to wealth and local prominence through Thomas Brassey, the leading railway contractor at a time when lines were being built all over the world; he was responsible for a significant proportion of them. It isn't clear why a family from Cheshire and having no southern connection should have moved to Sussex, but perhaps it was from a claim that an ancestor had come over with the Conqueror.

A driving force may have been his son, also Thomas. He was renting Beauport Park and presumably wanted somewhere of his own. By the mid-1860s the family set up a trust to undertake the mammoth task of building a house that would not only accommodate the family and its many servants but would also demonstrate its wealth and influence. The house was certainly big. But Normanhurst Court lasted for a shorter time than any other great house in the area. Built in 1869, it was demolished in 1951.

To describe the architecture of this very large house is difficult. It is a mixture of styles, the dominant one perhaps being French, of the period when the Loire châteaux were built. Its architects remained quiet if not embarrassed.

It is likely that they were Habershon, Spalding and Brock, particularly well-known in Sussex for their work on churches during the ecclesiastical building spree of the mid-century. One was St Andrew in Hastings, now demolished and replaced by Morrison's supermarket. Others are at Copthorne and Dallington. The RIBA has their initial plan for Normanhurst, dated 1862, which shows a much smaller house and one rather less influenced by the French renaissance. Another source suggests an odder designer: the quirky Frenchman Hector Horeau (1801–1872). He had already designed

Pippingford Manor on Ashdown Forest in a fairly restrained manner. He was to be more ambitious.

Normanhurst Court after enlargement in 1903,
photo origin unknown

For the Great Exhibition of 1851 he proposed a spherical design for what became the Crystal Palace, in quite impractical terms; and he also proposed an equally impractical cross-Channel railway in a submerged tube held in position by paddle steamers. It may be that Horeau provided the French influence on Normanhurst, distantly reminiscent of the châteaux of the Loire, but he seems not to have been further involved.

When completed Normanhurst had not only a covered tennis court (which became a military hospital in the First World War) but its own gas works. It employed a full-time interior decorator. The park was stocked with deer and at one point included a lonely emu gathered by Lady Brassey in Australia.

It was on *Sunbeam* that on a voyage to Mauritius his first wife had died of malaria in 1887 and had been buried at sea.

The eldest son Thomas lived at Normanhurst from its completion. He was a major force in the locality, including Hastings and elsewhere: an MP then a baron, Governor of Victoria, Australia (1895–1900), and an earl. He spent time cruising in various parts of the world on

The Brassey's yacht *Sunbeam*

Sunbeam. In 1918 he was succeeded by his only son, who died in a road accident only a year later.

There was no male heir and the daughters were comfortably married elsewhere (well, one of them had split from her husband and lived away from Sussex). They now had responsibility for a colossal house, surplus to requirements at a time when money was shorter than it had been and there were fewer young men of wealth to buy it, so many having died in the war; nor were servants so plentiful. The Countess moved to Park Dale and in 1920 Normanhurst and estate were put up for auction, but the house didn't sell. At the beginning of 1922 St Hilary's Girls' School moved there from Bexhill. As Normanhurst School it survived until the house was requisitioned in 1939.

The family remained locally prominent. The last Earl's wife Idina, daughter of the Marquess of Abergavenny, gave conspicuous service as a nurse in the First World War when Normanhurst provided its military hospital. The local connection continued through the first earl's daughters.

Mabelle married an Egerton and became châtelaine of Mountfield

Court. Muriel married Earl de la Warr, who engaged in a notorious affair with an actress for which she divorced him in 1902. She was a strong supporter of women's rights and a member of the Labour Party. Their son Herbrand became the ninth earl in 1915. After Eton he joined the Royal Navy and served on minesweepers to the end of the war; he was said to have been the only man ever to have stood on the steps of the throne in the uniform of an able-bodied seaman. As a major property owner in Bexhill and as mayor there (like his Brassey father before him) he was instrumental in creating the modernist pavilion that bears his name. Marie married a rising Liberal politician named Freeman Freeman-Thomas, who later became Governor-General of Canada and later Viceroy of India. He was created Marquess of Willingdon, the last creation of that rank outside the royal family. When she died in 1960 she left Swanborough Manor near Lewes to the then emerging University of Sussex, which controversially disposed of it in 1983.

Conditions after 1945 were much worse than after 1918. Normanhurst had been a barracks and then a prisoner-of-war camp, and its state must have been very bad. It was again put up for sale, and again there were no buyers. This was a time when many country houses were redundant and many knocked down. In 1951 it was demolished. The railway contractor must have dreamed of a dynasty based at Normanhurst but today one can see there only a caravan park.

The man who started the Boy Scouts and another who started the Boer War

Lord Edward Herbert Gascoyne-Cecil (1867–1918) and Alfred, Viscount Milner (1854–1925)

Cecil and Milner were connected to the Battle area through their marriage to the same woman and their residence (somewhat intermittently) at Great Wigsell, a country house a little south of Hawkhurst but in the parish of Salehurst and Robertsbridge.

Cecil, a son of the third Marquess of Salisbury, prime minister for twelve of the years between 1886 and 1902, owned Great Wigsell in the early twentieth century. It is unclear how much he lived there because he spent almost all of his life in other countries. His wife Violet, however, of whom more below, lived there until she died in 1958. Great Wigsell is a large, irregularly-shaped house, mainly early 17th century, restored by Sir Ernest George in 1905 after it had been unoccupied for some years.

Edward went for a military career but failed at Sandhurst. One can imagine that it was only his status that allowed him to be commissioned in the Grenadier Guards and establish a military reputation, fighting in Egypt and the Sudan. He was part of Kitchener's victorious army at Omdurman and then took part in Kitchener's expedition to Fashoda that resulted in the French leaving the Sudan. In 1899 Colonel Baden Powell engaged him as Chief

Staff Officer and they left for South Africa for what was to become known as the Second Boer War.

Cecil was notorious for his financial incapacity but in South Africa he triumphed. The inadequacy of the British army at that time is now famous.

It was generally under-provisioned, and unprepared for a long period of engagement. Believing that the war would last longer than did his over-confident colleagues, he saw a need for better supplies. The army would not produce them, so he personally guaranteed £500,000 and obtained them.

Although his commanding officer, Baden Powell, has been given the credit, it was Cecil's action in this respect that proved crucial in enabling the besieged town of Mafeking (now Mafekeng), to hold out until its famous relief. It was also Cecil's initiative, in setting up a group of boys as the Mafeking Cadet Corps, to carry messages, help in the hospital and perform other functions, that was to lead to the founding of what would become the Boy Scout Movement.

LORD EDWARD CECIL AND BOY SCOUT IN MAFEKING

Cecil kept close to Kitchener, who valued him although he was not appreciated by many senior leaders, now including Baden-Powell. This led him to Egypt, where he served in several governmental capacities.

In those days Egypt was in a curious position. The Ottoman empire still had some rather distant formal control but effectively it was a self-governing British colony where every department of state was subject to British observation and ultimately to British control. Among other posts he held there was that of Financial Adviser, which led to some mirth in his family. He continued even after Kitchener's untimely death in June 1916. In 1918 he was diagnosed with tuberculosis and went to Switzerland to recover. He died there, apparently of influenza, in December of that year.

In 1894 Cecil had made an unfortunate marriage to Violet Maxse, sister of Ivor Maxse who was to become one of the better British generals of the First World War. Although Cecil possessed great charm, Violet had more.

Moreover, she was talented in art and writing and was an attractive woman. Her marriage – which yielded a son killed in the first month of the First World War and commemorated on the Robertsbridge war memorial – was soon agreed by all to be unsatisfactory, and things got worse. She went to South Africa with her husband and at once fell under the spell, which was reciprocated, of Alfred Milner.

Violet Gascoyne-Cecil is on the left; Milner is seated next to her; next to him is Joseph Chamberlain. Cecil may be the man standing behind her left shoulder. From Cecil Headlam, *The Milner Papers*, 1899–1905, London: Butler & Tanner, 1933.

This may have happened as early as 1900, for in 1901 she and another woman founded the Victoria League to promote Milner's view of the British empire. This still exists as a significant charitable body with branches in Australia, and New Zealand and affiliated organisations in Canada and (not oddly for the time) the USA. After her husband's death Violet was free to marry him, which she did in 1921, and both lived at Great Wigsell.

Though a British nationalist, Milner was partly of German descent and had been born at Giessen, a little north of Frankfurt-am-Main. He had a most successful time at Oxford and was then called to the Bar. He spent time in the civil service in Egypt before being appointed chairman of the Board of the Inland Revenue. He so impressed politicians that in 1897 he became High Commissioner for Southern Africa and Governor of the Cape Colony.

Milner was a prime mover of the South African war of 1899–1902. He was a brilliant if outspoken imperialist who pushed the Colonial Secretary Joseph Chamberlain into making demands that the Afrikaner leaders of the Transvaal were certain to reject.

He had quickly formed the view that there could be no compromise with the Afrikaner-controlled Transvaal, which continued to refuse any rights to the large numbers of Britons there, who were primarily involved in mining operations. If they were allowed full rights they would come to dominate the Afrikaners.

Milner met President Kruger and made demands that anyone could see were unacceptable. Kruger must have felt under enormous pressure. His men had stopped the Jameson raid into the Transvaal at the turn of 1895/96, but to take on the whole British empire was a much bigger matter. Nevertheless he was famously a stubborn and principled man and he held out. The consequence was war and a compromise peace that, however, insisted on British control of the Transvaal and the Orange Free State; Milner was governor of both before leaving South Africa in 1905.

Milner was by this time very much a Conservative. Whatever his views, he was a valuable man to have at one's side and he joined Lloyd George's War Cabinet at the end of 1916 as Secretary of State for War, thereafter working hard for an effective victory and being crucial in the 1918 decision of the Allies to have a single command.

He was key to the writing of the Balfour Declaration of 1917; that he thus contributed to Middle Eastern politics may or may not be praiseworthy. He was to be Secretary of State for the Colonies. He was awarded a viscountcy and the Order of the Garter.

South Africa got the end of him, though. Visiting there in 1925 he contracted sleeping sickness and soon died.

Violet, now twice a widow, lived on at Great Wigsell to her death in 1958, active in the defence of her property against those wishing to designate footpaths across it. For some years from 1932 she edited the Conservative periodical, the *National Review,* in succession to her brother. Both she and her second husband are buried in Salehurst churchyard.

Her house was then sold. It remains in private hands.

12
Odd people out

The three people here leave questions behind them: who was he, was he really as old as his tombstone claims and did she really leave a queen's jewels here?

An astrologist and doctor

❦

Edmund Langdon
(dates unknown)

L angdon was the first known scientist of Battle, someone of whom we know almost nothing – except that his 'science' was worthless.

He wrote from Battle in 1610 that he was a 'general practitioner in astronomie and physicke', but further evidence is lacking. Langdon's methods, according to his own printed notebook of some 140 pages, derived from the monthly position of the planets, by no means all of which had by then been identified.

This is as if nowadays we treated patients by reference to the signs of the zodiac. His beliefs were not unusual for those days, though whether his diagnoses were correct or his treatments effective we do not know. If they were then it was almost certainly accidental.

Similar in their approach were the well-known Nicolas Culpeper (1816–54) and Elias Ashmole (1617–92, whose collections form the basis of the Ashmolean Museum at Oxford and include Langdon's notebook. Some old treatments did appear to work but no-one appears to have carried out proper tests. They relied on ancient texts instead. Indeed, modern scientific methods reliant on tests did not gain hold until after the work of Francis Bacon shortly after Langdon's notebook. Bacon proposed proper, repeated and reliable testing, and his approach forms the basis of the scientific approach today.

Did Isaac Ingall really die at the age of 120?

Isaac Ingall
(?–1798)

I ngall remains one of Battle's best-known characters, if only because he is reputed to have died at the age of 120. It is carved into his gravestone in the churchyard so it must be true. But is it? And who was he?

Ingall was a servant of the Webster family at Battle Abbey who rose to become the head of the staff and, according to contemporary accounts, was well known both for his longevity and his short temper.

The Duchess of Cleveland, writing several decades later, paints a vivid picture:

> .... He insisted on holding this post of honour almost to the very last, and used to bring up bottles of wine after dinner, suspended between his trembling old fingers, clinking together like so many castanets. But no-one liked to interfere with him, for always cross and testy, his temper did not mellow with his years, and he grew more and more difficult to deal with as time went by, and left him behind.

John Byng, when visiting the abbey in 1788, reported that he

> caught a glimpse of the lofty old hall and one old chamber; and saw yet a greater curiosity, the family butler, Mr Ingall, 103 years of age, who had been a post-boy in York in Queen Anne's reign, and now frequently, in a passion, gives warnings and threatened to leave his place. He was very deaf, else I would have spoken to him; but we both bowed to him, and his age bowed to us!

M.ʳ Isaac Ingall . aged 116 Years

"An Antient and Faithful domestic to the
Family at Battle Abbey where he now lives
having been nearly 90 years in its service"
Sir Godfrey Vassall Webster caused this Portrait
to be drawn as a memorial of this Venerable Man.

Died on 2ⁿᵈ April 1798 aged 120 years

Isaac Ingall, from Battle Abbey estate, date unknown

Nearly ten years later, an account in the *Gentleman's Magazine* of November 1797 describes how the writer travelled sixty miles in the snow to see Ingall. It seems pretty clear that the old gentleman was not unaccustomed to similar visits, and that he cordially disliked them. He seemed to be remarkably spry for his age.

> There was nothing in his look which impressed on the mind the idea of a person more than almost fourscore [80] years old, except a falling of his under jaw, which bespoke his more advanced age.... In each of his withered hands he held a short rude walking-stick about three feet high, by the help of which he was accustomed not only to walk about the extensive premises in which he passed his life, but to take his little rambles about the town....

Shortly before his death he was visited by Prince William of Gloucester, who presented him with a pound of the best Scotch [snuff] accompanied by a one pound banknote, gifts that he apparently received with great pleasure.

He was undoubtedly very old at the time of his death, but the question is just how old?

Byng's report of him in 1788 states that he had been a servant with the Webster family for nearly 90 years; newspaper reports on his death in 1798 give his age as one hundred and twenty and attribute to him nearly ninety-five years of service with the Websters. If Byng's account above is correct, by 1798 Ingall would have been 'only' 113, certainly very old but within reach.

Claims of great age were not unusual before the official recording of births, marriages and deaths. In the mid-nineteenth century it was said in Burwash that there was a man of 160 fit enough to take part in hop-picking. Tom Parr of Shropshire is well-known because it was claimed that he died at the age of 152 in 1635. The *Hastings and St Leonards Observer* in 1919 recorded a grave at Salehurst claiming that Peter Sparkes died there in 1683 at the age of 126, though it does say that the gravestone was hard to read; further investigation for the Sussex Family History Group suggests 120. Both are at best improbable.

We know little to be able either to substantiate or to deny the claim of 120 years, though if the contemporary accounts are to be believed Ingall must have been at least 100. It is clear that his wife died about 60 years before him, being buried at Battle on 9 December 1751.

The answer to the question depends on finding exactly who he was and where he came from. If Ingall had been in the Websters' service for some 90 years in about 1791, then he was not of Battle because Webster did not arrive at Battle until 1721. One must look for him elsewhere.

On 1701, those ninety years before 1788, when he supposedly came into their employment, the Websters were living at Copt Hall in Essex, being of Fenchurch St, London and Nelmes, Havering, Essex before then.

If there are records of Ingall's birth or residence, then perhaps they might be found in Essex or London parishes. However, the records so far accessed contained no London or Essex births of an Isaac Ingall of the right kind of age.

There is elsewhere, however, one baptism of precisely the right alleged age: at Braithwell, Yorkshire on 29 July 1677. Braithwell is near Maltby, close to Nottinghamshire. Yorkshire might seem a little far away from Essex or London to be a convincing source for the old man but there could have been a connection between the Websters and that area. Sir Thomas, the first Webster to own the Abbey, came from Chesterfield in Derbyshire, only some 40 miles away from Braithwell and the Duchess of Cleveland found that the northern/north Midlands origins of the Websters are clear, as was some continuing connection with the area. Does this support the suggestion that Ingall was born at Braithwell in 1677? Unfortunately, back in those early days local records were often sketchy and incomplete or have been lost.

So we have a record of someone of the correct name whose date of baptism fits the reputed age of the old man. It is possible that our Isaac Ingall was, indeed, the one born at Braithwell in 1677, in which case perhaps he was 120 after all. But doubts must remain. For example, in 1788 Byng reported that Ingall was a post-boy at York 'in the reign of Queen Anne' (1702–14) which seems late for one born in 1677, who would have been in his late twenties and early thirties, but less so for one born ten years or so later. Moreover, if Ingall had joined the Websters in the south in about 1701 he could not have been a postboy in the reign of Queen Anne.

And there is a record of him having a child in 1762/63 when (if 120 is true) he would already have been about 85: not impossible but unlikely. Similarly, it appears that the mother would have been only 27 at the time of conception: perhaps an unlikely union. There were also long visits to the North when he was apparently at a very advanced age, no doubt rather trying for a man so old.

Some people think that maybe Ingall may have been about 100 when he died. If Byng was correct in saying that Ingall was 103 in 1788, then he was 113 when he died, and this may be the truth. Men have been reliably recorded as reaching this age. Given the paucity and imprecision of available records, it is hardly surprising that no birth can be found for him in about 1685.

So the mystery remains. It seems that we shall never know and the case stays open.

The Princess and the jewels

Princesse Marie Teresa Louise de Lamballe
(1749–1792)

There is a persistent story – persistent, that is, because of repetition over the past two centuries – that some of the jewels of Queen Marie Antoinette of France were brought to Catsfield for safe keeping in 1791. The courier was her trusted friend the Princesse de Lamballe. The story does not seem to have been mentioned by any of the British newspapers, so its origins are unclear.

Marie Louise had little luck in her life of nearly 43 years. She was a member of a junior branch of the house of Savoy, which many years after her premature death ended up as kings of Sardinia and then of Italy. At the age of 17 she was married off to an extraordinarily wealthy descendant of the French royal family who very soon died of venereal disease. The Prince de Lamballe had been named after the town close to the north coast of Normandy, today dominated by its spectacular cathedral. He was a descendant of Louis XIV and the heir to what was reckoned to be the greatest fortune in France.

The French royal family rescued the widow, and she became a close friend of Marie Antoinette of Austria, who had married the heir to the French throne at the then common age of 14; she became queen in 1774, when she was 18. Fifteen years later the French Revolution broke out, though it didn't become more than occasionally violent for a little while.

For the royal family the turning point was in June 1791. They tried to flee the country but were intercepted at Varennes-en-Argonne in north-eastern France, close to where foreign troops were

216

Madame la princesse de Lamballe by Antoine-François Callet (about 1776). Museum of the History of France, Versailles, Public Domain CCO 1.0)

based, and they were brought back to Paris. It was now obvious to all revolutionaries that the royals opposed the principles of the revolution and were prepared to fight to restore the old order of autocracy and privilege.

For the Princess the change of mood was a disaster. She may just have been responsible for trying to safeguard at least some of Marie Antoinette's jewels. When she came to England she lived for a short time at Bath, but also is reported to have come to Catsfield where the Gibbs family then owned Catsfield Place. Sir Vicary Gibbs was a well-known barrister and MP, knighted in 1805, who rose to be Solicitor-General then Attorney-General, ending as Lord Chief Justice. It is possible, indeed likely, that the Princess and the then

Mrs Gibbs had met at Bath, a most popular centre of recreation for the upper classes.

Contemporary reports suggest that she and a colleague came to England to persuade the King to make war on France, and there is another reference to her being here at the invitation of the Duchess of Devonshire. None mention jewels. The Duchess, being married to a major Sussex landowner, might have been the conduit to the Catsfield owners.

In 1792 Austria declared war on France ostensibly, but very misguidedly, for the safety of the French royal family whose queen was Austrian. It prepared to attack from what is now Belgium.

War made the French royal family the likely enemies of their country and they were imprisoned. The Princess went back to Paris to support the Queen and joined her in prison; she was quickly regarded as a figurehead of resistance. No doubt the revolutionaries knew of her journey to England as well as her closeness to the royal family. Moreover she was not French.

On 3 September 1792 she was brought to court in what would later, mildly, be called a show trial. She proclaimed herself in favour of liberty, conveniently undefined; but when asked to swear hatred to the royal family she decently refused. She was immediately taken off to be killed, and the mob outside carried out the sentence. Published details of her death are particularly disturbing but may owe some exaggeration to opponents of the revolution wishing to show how unpleasant its adherents were. Opinions vary whether September 1792 was the beginning of the 'reign of terror' but that month was the first in which massacres took place. The King and Queen went to the guillotine in the following year.

We do not know whether the jewels sold by Sotheby's in 2019 were the only ones that had been missing. If not, that brings us back to the question: if the jewels were taken to Catsfield where are they now? No indication of their whereabouts, let alone a sight, has ever been had. Of course, if someone had found them, they might well have disposed of them discreetly and for large sums of money. No-one knows. If they are still at Catsfield (if indeed they ever were) perhaps some later generation will unearth them.

Sources

This book could not have been produced without the following articles available on the BDHS website at www. battlehistorysociety.com. The codes in the table below indicate the position of the articles in Collectanea there. The articles contain references omitted from this book. Any further information in the book has been added by the editor.

Code	Title	Author(s)
A 3.1	Abbots, abbeys and priories	Keith Foord
A 4.4	Eastern Sussex under the Norman and Angevin kings of England	Keith Foord
A 4.6	Eastern Sussex 1327–1461, from Edward III to Henry VI's deposition	Keith Foord
C 8.1	The banks of Battle	George Kiloh
D 1.1	Physicians of Battle to 1945	George Kiloh
D 4.1	The Battle Union Workhouse	Adrian and Sarah Hall
E 2.1	Cresy Report of 1850 (original report)	General Board of Health
F 3.5	William Vidler – a Peculiar clergyman	Keith Foord
F 4.1	The history of Battle's Catholic Church	Keith Foord
F 4.2	Thomas Pilcher, Battle-born martyr	Keith Foord
F 4.3	Brownes, Montagus and recusancy	Keith Foord, Adrian and Sarah Hall
H 1.1	Members of Parliament who have covered Battle and District	George Kiloh
H 3.1	Battle and William Cobbett	Adrian and Sarah Hall
H 4.1	Barbara Bodichon – women's rights	Adrian and Sarah Hall
H 4.2	Guy Hayler – alcohol abolitionist	George Kiloh

Particular note should be taken of these books:

Conquest to Dissolution 1067–1538, by Keith Foord, includes an account of the abbots of Battle Abbey and similar establishments, as well as pre-dissolution kingly activities in the area.

Hancox – a House and a Family by Charlotte Moore, a compelling account of the family of Sir Norman Moore, Barbara Bodichon and Ben Leigh Smith and of the house at Whatlington.

Dadland by Tom Carew's daughter Keggie cannot be too highly recommended.

Battle Abbey and the Websters by Roy Pryce is the most thorough account of a troubled dynasty.

Edmund Langdon and his World, by Adrian and Sarah Hall, is a thorough investigation of this largely-hidden astrologer.

A Life of Fire, Stephen Crane by Paul Sorrentino is a fine biography of this challenging author.

Hemingfold by John Shepperd, a full account of the area near the south end of Battle parish.

Some information has come from *The Brave Remembered: Battle at War 1914–1919*, written by the present editor, from *The Pelican History of Canada*, by Kenneth McNaught, for the quotation from James Murray and from *Fitzroy* by John and Mary Gribbin.

Newspapers: in particular the *Sussex Weekly Advertiser*, the *Hastings and St Leonards Observer* and the *Sussex Express* have all yielded useful data, through www.britishnewspaperarchive.co.uk. Some use has been made of entries in www.ancestry.co.uk.

Index

❦

Names of people featured are in bold type.

Lightning Source UK Ltd.
Milton Keynes UK
UKHW051551080822
406998UK00014B/625

9 781903 099100